THE GREAT AMERICAN HISTORY BOOK EVER…
EVER…
EVER…
EVER…

PART ONE

Peter Dietz

Pete Remenicky

800lb Lemur Publishing

Text and Illustration COPYRIGHT 2015 by Peter Dietz and Peter Remenicky

All characters listed as "Some of Our Friends" and all related icons are included in this copyright.

No part of this publication may be reproduced in whole or in part, or stored in a retrieval system, or transmitted in any form or by any means, electronic, mechanical, photocopying, recording, or otherwise.

All rights reserved.

Library of Congress Registration Number: TXu 1-965-347

800lb Lemur Publishing LLC

ISBN-13: 978-0692619421
ISBN-10: 0692619429

Find us at **www.greatesthistorybookever.com.**

Follow **greatesthistorybookever** on Instagram.

Like **The Greatest History Book Ever** on Facebook.

For Ofer Sankowski,

Miss Ya, Buddy.

For Purdy, Birdy, and the Bammer,

Thanks for the love and support.

Who We Are:

I'm me, he's him...which make us we. I promise that the remainder of this book will not be as confusing as its first sentence. Three years ago, I (me, the social studies guy) went to him (the art guy) and asked him how he learned history because he reminded me of some of our students. He is very intelligent, but he learns differently than I do. He told me that he doodled all of his notes, labeled the notes, and reviewed the doodles and words together. He showed me how it looked, I added some words, and an idea was born.

One thing I want to make clear: WE ARE TEACHERS. I (me again) love the history stuff, he (him) loves art, and we created this book with very little magical power in order to help you review, reinforce, and recall historical information to make you a better American History student. We are experienced teachers who have worked in high school and middle school, in traditional learning environments and alternative schools. This is not a psychology experiment, and it is not a test; it only serves to give you a different way to gain valuable knowledge, improve your grades, and gain confidence.

Thanks bunches,

Peter and Pete

MEMORY HOOKS

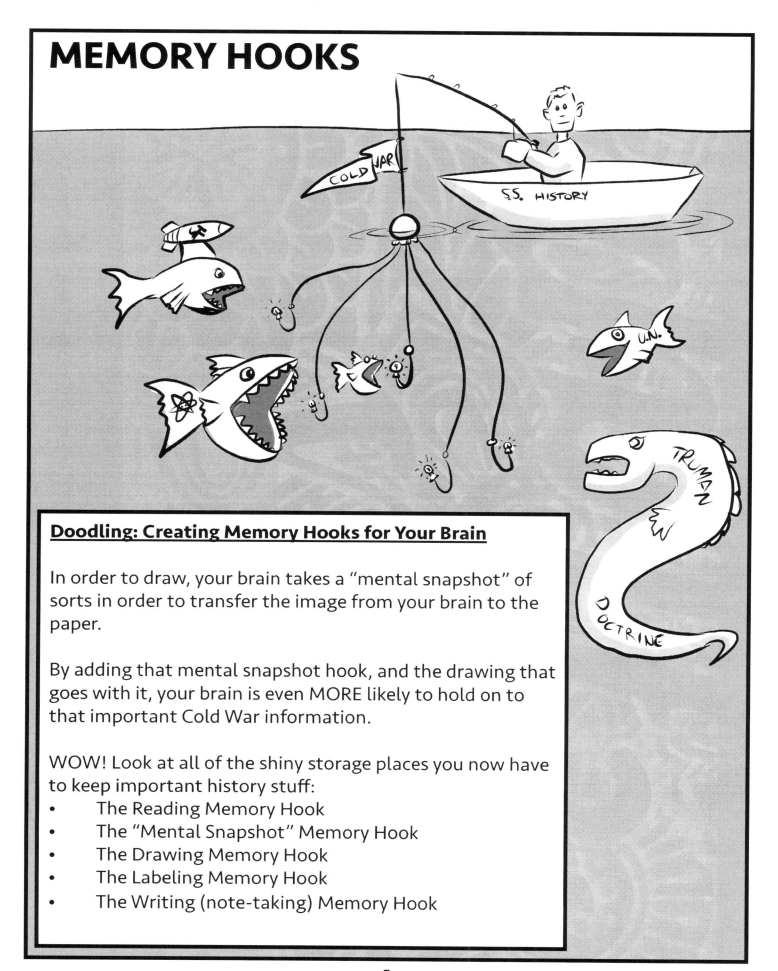

Doodling: Creating Memory Hooks for Your Brain

In order to draw, your brain takes a "mental snapshot" of sorts in order to transfer the image from your brain to the paper.

By adding that mental snapshot hook, and the drawing that goes with it, your brain is even MORE likely to hold on to that important Cold War information.

WOW! Look at all of the shiny storage places you now have to keep important history stuff:
- The Reading Memory Hook
- The "Mental Snapshot" Memory Hook
- The Drawing Memory Hook
- The Labeling Memory Hook
- The Writing (note-taking) Memory Hook

DIRECTIONS

WARNING You DO NOT have to be artistic for this book to be effective. It is the process that increases your ability to remember important historical information. Do the best you can. ☺

STEP 1: <u>Read</u> the write-up on the left. (Out LOUD is great!)

STEP 2: <u>Look</u> at our doodle, label the various symbols, and a take a few notes in the thin blank space between our doodle and your drawing area. We only left a small note-taking space as a reminder to take notes on ONLY the most important material.

* NOTE: Anytime you see a pencil, you are expected to add information in the space provided.

STEP 3: <u>Draw</u> the doodle as best you can in the space provided. Some doodles give you a bit of an outline to help you manage the space. Try to doodle at a steady pace: The drawing aspect of this is NOT meant to be a time vampire.

STEP 4: <u>Review</u> your doodles and notes for a couple of minutes per day in order to firmly fasten those events, people, laws, etc. onto as many memory hooks in your brain as possible. <u>Add</u> to the drawing or write-up if you would like. You are the author and the artist.

Meet Some of Our Friends

Factory

Who I Am: Industry, corporations, or industrialization

Likes: Big $$, capitalism, cheap labor, and de-regulation

Dislikes: Government regulation, labor shortages, unions, and corporate taxes

Friends: Lazy Fairy, national bank, railroads, and captains of industry

Foes: Striking workers

Where You Might Find Me: A doodle about immigration, sectionalism, or nationalization

Safe

Who I Am: Banking in the US

Likes: Big $$, capitalism, industry, railroads

Dislikes: Government regulation, stock market crashes, and runs on me

Friends: Alexander Hamilton, Lazy Fairy, and Ronald Reagan

Foes: Glass-Steagall Act, recessions, and depressions

Where You Might Find Me: A doodle about *McCulloch v. MD* (1819), the New Deal, or Reaganomics

Power Eagle

Who I Am: The expansion of federal power

Likes: Federalism, the Constitution

Dislikes: Articles of Confederation, Shays' Rebellion

Friends: John Marshall, Alexander Hamilton, and Abraham Lincoln

Foes: Anti-Federalists and anyone who wants to get "power-eagled"

Where You Might Find Me: A doodle on the Marshall Court or nationalization

Uncle Sam

Who I Am: The federal government and America

Likes: America, Americans, and freedom

Dislikes: Soviet bears, the 3/5 Compromise, and teachers and other adults who fret about the fact that Uncle Sam appears on doodles which are linked to time periods when the icon of Uncle Sam had yet to be created. Congrats to you, smarty-pants. This book also features a hawk carrying a pistol and a giant safe walking on a tightrope. It's supposed to be fun…loosen up.

Friends: Power Eagles, Bill of Rights, and the Constitution

Foes: Anything that threatens America or limits the rights of Americans

Where You Might Find Me: A doodle about the Civil War, the Civil Rights Movement, or the Cold War

GET OFF MY LAWN! Guy
(Must be attempted using your best New York City accent)

Who I Am: Isolationism, nativism, or both

Likes: Quotas, Exclusion Acts, Monroe Doctrine, Neutrality Acts

Dislikes: Unlimited immigration, new immigrants, European intervention, and World Wars

Friends: Nativists, Know-Nothings, KKK, union leaders, isolationism, James Monroe

Foes: Businesses looking for cheap labor, War Hawk, Red Scary

Where You Might Find Me: A doodle for the Monroe Doctrine, Immigration, or American neutrality prior to WWII

Wrench

Who I Am: Reforms or reformers which created positive change for average Americans

Likes: Forward thinking and expansion of rights

Dislikes: Monopolies, nativists, and meanies

Friends: Jane Addams, Teddy Roosevelt, Dorothea Dix, Horace Mann, Booker T. Washington, and W.E.B. DuBois

Foes: Jim Crow and robber barons

Where You Might Find Me: A doodle regarding progressivism

Fraidy Cat

Who I Am: Eras, events, people, and policies which scared Americans

Likes: Stability and conflict-free living

Dislikes: The teachers who want to remind me that my name is NOT a real word. I have enough to worry about without having to endure an identity crisis. Fraidy is a family name…let it go.

Friends: Peace Dove, but I trust no one.

Foes: War Hawk, rebellions, nukes, and satellites

Where You Might Find Me: A doodle in the build-up to the Civil War or the Cold War

Peace Dove

Who I Am: Events, people, and policies which promote peace and harmony

Likes: Non-violent protests, treaties, and détente

Dislikes: War, radicalism, and violence

Friends: Hippies, Fraidy Cat, Martin Luther King, Jr., Cesar Chavez, and groovy people

Foes: War Hawk, Jim Crow, and meanies

Where You Might Find Me: A doodle during Reconstruction, Vietnam protests, or the Cold War

Crow

Who I Am: The segregationist policies of the Jim Crow South

Likes: Segregation, racism, oppression, and lack of voting rights for Blacks

Dislikes: Civil rights, marches, sit-ins, and equality

Friends: KKK and segregationists

Foes: Dr. King, Student Non-Violent Coordinating Committee (SNCC), and Rosa Parks

Where You Might Find Me: A doodle from the Reconstruction Era, Civil Rights Movement, or affirmative action

Lazy Fairy

Who I Am: Laissez-faire economics and those who agree with government de-regulation

Likes: Railroads, big businesses, and the de-regulation of corporations

Dislikes: Unions, the Grange, government intervention, the New Deal, and the Great Society

Friends: Herbert Hoover, captains of industry, and Ronald Reagan

Foes: International Workers of the World (IWW), American Federation of Labor, Franklin D. Roosevelt, Lyndon B. Johnson, and Barack Obama

Where You Might Find Me: A doodle from the Gilded Age, Manifest Destiny, and New Deal

Red Scary

Who I Am: The Red Scare (1st during the 1920s and 2nd during the early Cold War era); I am the communist threat to the US.

Likes: Communism, nativism, fear, unions, and the USSR

Dislikes: Democracy, freedom, and capitalism

Friends: Sacco and Vanzetti, anarchists, and labor agitators

Foes: GET OFF MY LAWN! Guy, nativists, and Joseph McCarthy

Where You Might Find Me: A doodle on the 1920s or the Early Cold War

Other Stuff You are Going to See

 The **barn and silo** represent family farms.

 The **peach** represents impeachment proceedings.

 The **balloon** represents that something is on the RISE.

 The **anarchy symbol** represents anarchists who fight against authority.

The Greatest Table of Contents Ever...Ever...Ever...Ever

Chapter 1: Europeans Who Said, "Thou," "Thus," and "Hath" Who Became Americans Who Said, "Thou," "Thus," and "Hath"

16. Jamestown Settlement and the Massachusetts Bay Colony
18. Mayflower Compact: 1620
20. Colonial America: Northern Economy v. Southern Economy
22. French and Indian War: 1754 - 1763
24. The Boston Massacre: 1770
26. The Boston Tea Party: 1773
28. The Intolerable Acts: 1774
30. The Battles of Lexington and Concord: 1775
32. *Common Sense*: 1776
34. The Declaration of Independence: 1776
36. The British Surrender at Yorktown: 1781

Chapter 2: American Government — We Make a Rough Draft and Leave Some Room for Editing

38. Examples of American Democracy
40. The Weaknesses of the Articles of Confederation: 1781
42. Northwest Ordinance: 1787
44. Shays' Rebellion: 1786 - 1787
46. The Constitutional Convention: 1787
48. Federalists v. Anti-Federalists: 1787 - 1789
50. The Great Compromise: 1787
52. 3/5 Compromise: 1787
54. Preamble / Powers of the Three Branches
56. Federalism (The Federal System)
58. Checks and Balances
60. Unwritten Constitution
62. The Bill of Rights: 1791

Chapter 3: Hatching the Power Eagle

64. Jefferson's America v. Hamilton's America
66. The Whiskey Rebellion: 1794
68. George Washington's Farewell Address (Essay): 1796
70. John Adams — A Troubled Presidency : 1797 - 1801
72. Louisiana Purchase: 1803
74. The Lewis and Clark Expedition: 1804 - 1806
76. *Marbury v. Madison*: 1803
78. *McCulloch v. Maryland*: 1819
80. *Gibbons v. Ogden*: 1824
82. War of 1812

Chapter 4: America Takes Some "Me" Time

84. Monroe Doctrine: 1823
86. Andrew Jackson and the Rise of Executive Power: 1829 - 1837
88. Andrew Jackson and the Spoils System
90. Andrew Jackson and the Nullification Crisis: 1832
92. Indian Removal Act and the Trail of Tears: 1830 - 1831
94. The Alamo and the Mexican-American War: 1836 - 1848
96. Seneca Falls Convention: 1848
98. Susan B. Anthony
100. Dorothea Dix
102. Horace Mann

Chapter 5: Kinda Angry about Slavery to Super Duper Angry About Slavery

104. Sectionalism
106. Missouri Compromise: 1820
108. Nat Turner's Slave Rebellion: 1831
110. Frederick Douglass
112. The Underground Railroad
114. Harriet Beecher Stowe — *Uncle Tom's Cabin*: 1852
116. Sojourner Truth
118. Compromise of 1850
120. Kansas-Nebraska Act: 1854 / Bleeding Kansas: 1856
122. The Dred Scott Decision: 1857
124. John Brown's Raid on Harper's Ferry: 1859
126. Election of 1860

Chapter 6: The Most Violent Event in American History Which We Continue to Re-Enact Every Weekend

128. The Attack on Fort Sumter: 1861
130. Lincoln and the Income Tax: 1861
132. Lincoln and the Expansion of Executive Power: 1861 - 1865
134. Battle of Antietam: 1862
136. Emancipation Proclamation: 1863
138. Civil War Draft Riots: 1863
140. "Gettysburg Address": 1863
142. Sherman's March to the Sea: 1864

Chapter 7: A Couple Steps Forward, a Couple Steps Back

144. Reconstruction Plans: Lincoln's Plan v. Radical Republicans' Plan
146. The Assassination of Abraham Lincoln: 1865
148. Impeachment of President Andrew Johnson: 1868
150. The Formation of the KKK: 1866
152. The Civil War Amendments — 13th, 14th, and 15th
154. Freedmen's Bureaus: 1865 - 1872
156. Jim Crow Voting Laws
158. *Plessy v. Ferguson*: 1896
160. Booker T. Washington and W.E.B. Dubois

Chapter 8: America Moves Leftward

162. Manifest Destiny: Mid - Late 1800s
164. Transcontinental Railroad: 1862 - 1869
166. Homestead Act: 1862
168. The Dawes Act: 1887
170. The Grange
172. *Munn v. Illinois*: 1877
174. American Populism

Chapter 9: Mo' Money...Mo' Labor Disputes

176. Robber Barons or Captains of Industry
178. American Innovators at the Turn of the Century
180. Haymarket Affair: 1886
182. Rise of Major Unions at the Turn of the Century
184. Union Turmoil at the Turn of the Century
186. Political Machines of the Late 19th Century
188. Triangle Shirtwaist Fire: 1911

Chapter 10: Send Us Your Huddled Masses to Stop Sending Us Your Huddled Masses

190. US Immigration: 1870 - 1920
192. New Immigrants v. Old Immigrants: 1870 - 1920
194. Nativism — The Anti-Immigration Movement
196. Chinese Exclusion Act: 1882
198. Gentlemen's Agreement: 1907
200. Emergency Quota Act: 1921 / National Origins Act: 1924

Chapter 1

Chapter 1:

Europeans Who Said, "Thou," "Thus," and "Hath," Who Became

AMERICANS WHO SAID, "THOU," "THUS," AND "HATH"

Jamestown Settlement and the Massachusetts Bay Colony

Jamestown

- In the spring of 1607, a small group of merchants and mercenaries came from England to the coast of present day Virginia. They were instructed by Elizabeth I to search for precious metals and a water route to the Pacific Ocean.

- The group fell on hard times, suffering from illness and hunger, before agreeing to trade with the Powatan tribe which was native to that area.

- The Jamestown Settlement became profitable when the settlers turned their attention away from mining and exploration and began producing tobacco.

Massachusetts Bay

- In 1620, a group of English settlers landed on the tip of present-day Cape Cod, MA, before settling near present-day Plymouth, MA.

- Some of the settlers were from the English Separatist Church, a group of radical Puritans hoping to pursue a devout Christian life, free from government interventions. During the voyage, a group of Puritan men signed the Mayflower Compact, which became the framework for the first formal government of the colony.

- After suffering the hardships associated with Massachusetts winters, a second wave of Puritans arrived in 1630 to create a "City Upon a Hill." This group intended to model pure Christian living for the rest of the world.

- Though the relationship between the Puritans and the various tribes of the Wampanoag people has been portrayed as amicable, it was often characterized by violence and manipulation.

Link it Back

Many of the Puritans who came to Massachusetts were there because they protested against Elizabeth I's moderate religious policies, which called for tolerance in the division between Puritans and Catholics in England.

Link it Forward

Peaceful relations in Jamestown included the marriage of colonist John Rolfe to Pocahontas, the daughter of an Algonquin tribal leader, in 1614.

JAMESTOWN SETTLEMENT AND THE MASSACHUSETTS BAY COLONY

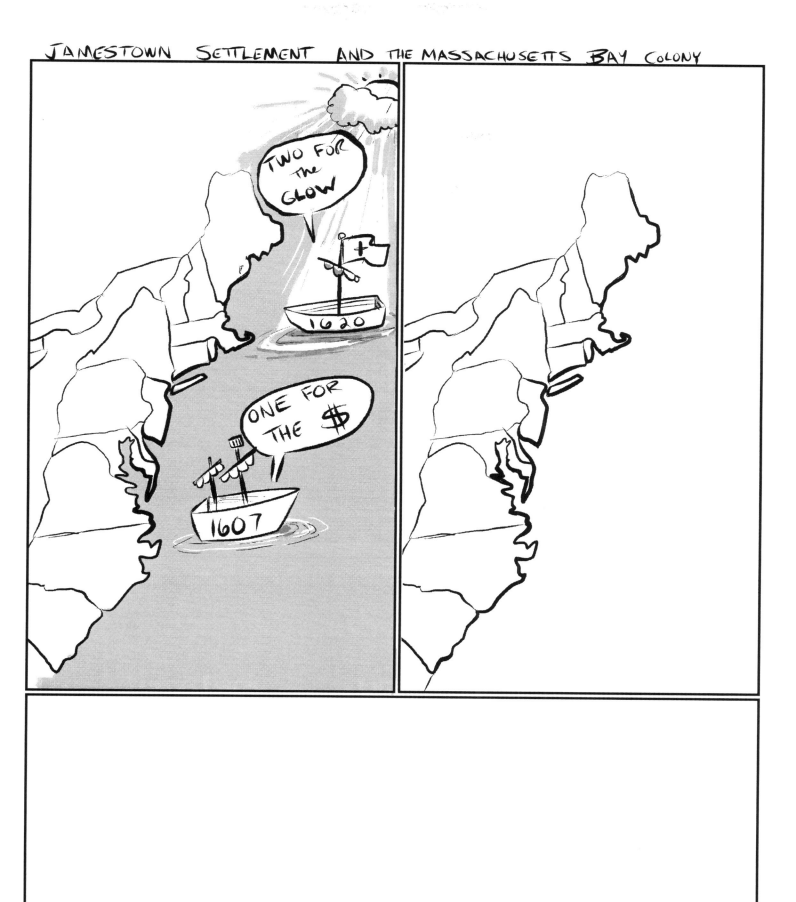

Mayflower Compact: 1620

- The Mayflower Compact was a set of laws and policies created by the pilgrims aboard the Mayflower while on their journey to the New World. This government structure was used in the Massachusetts Bay Colony to ensure "just and equal laws."

- This plan for government relied upon popular sovereignty, which stressed voting for male landholding citizens who would create laws and policies.

- The document helped to create a government which pledged loyalty to the king, but it became a landmark in the development of American democracy.

Link it Back

With the Virginia House of Burgesses already established as a democratic entity in the Jamestown Colony, the Compact became the link to democracy for pilgrims in the Massachusetts Bay Colony.

Link it Forward

Historians credit the Mayflower Compact as being the first set of written laws for European settlers in the New World. Founding fathers, such as John Adams, cited the Compact as the basis of the US Constitution.

MAYFLOWER COMPACT: 1620

Colonial America: Northern Economy v. Southern Economy

- The northern agricultural system consisted primarily of small to mid-size family farms.

- Cities in the northern colonies, such as New York and Boston, were centers of trade and industry.

- On the other hand, southern farming often centered around massive plantations which featured:

    ✓ Production of cash crops (often tobacco or cotton).

    ✓ The need for a massive labor force (indentured servants and slaves).

    ✓ A "Triangle Trade" which brought slaves to America, raw materials to Europe, and manufactured goods to Africa and the Americas.

    - The "Middle Passage" was the portion of the triangle that brought slaves to the Americas under horrible conditions.

- Industry in the South was very limited.

Link it Back

The Jamestown Colony, founded in 1607, began the tradition of a predominantly agrarian (agriculturally-based) economy in the southern colonies.

Link it Forward

The northern industrial centers were a major advantage for the Union Army in their battle against the Confederates in the Civil War of the mid-1800s.

COLONIAL AMERICA: NORTHERN ECONOMY V. SOUTHERN ECONOMY

French and Indian War: 1754 - 1763

- The French and Indian War pitted the French, who were supported by many Native American tribes, against the British, who were supported by northern colonists.

- As with many conflicts in the New World, the battle was essentially over land and trade. In this case, the valuable trade routes were in the Ohio River Valley.

- The British suffered multiple defeats until they gained the support of powerful Native American tribes. The British supplemented their forces with experienced commanders and soldiers in 1757, which allowed them to claim victory in 1763.

- The *Treaty of Paris* was an agreement that ceded (gave) control of virtually all of North America, east of the Mississippi River, to the British.

- The Proclamation of 1763 prohibited colonists from settling west of the Appalachian Mountains in order to prevent future land conflicts with Native Americans. The Proclamation was widely ignored by white settlers who moved westward to seek space for farming.

- Heavy taxation resulted from the costly French and Indian War. Colonists were upset that they fought for the British, paid significant taxes to the British, and were then prohibited by the British from moving westward after the war.

- British soldiers with lesser ranks not only gave orders to Colonial commanders, but also received superior pay. The war demonstrated to colonists that they were second class subjects of the king.

Link it Back

This was the fourth land conflict between the French and the British in the New World.

Link it Forward

Colonial officers, like George Washington, used their experiences from the French and Indian War to battle the British during the Revolutionary War.

FRENCH AND INDIAN WAR: 1754-1763

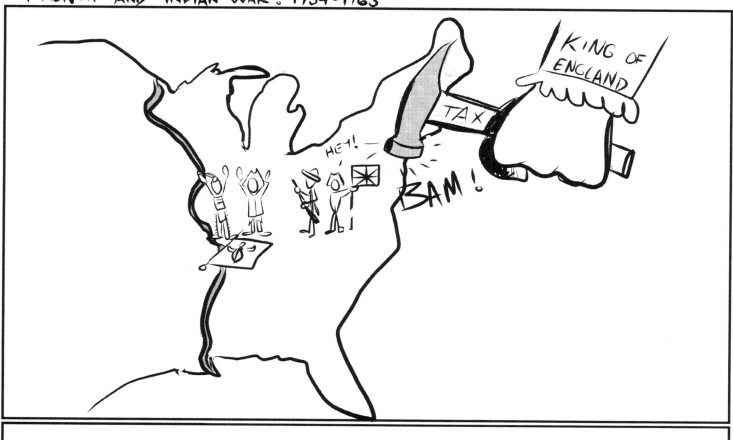

The Boston Massacre: 1770

- Colonists had multiple disputes with British soldiers and customs officers at the Port of Boston. Some of the issues at stake were shipping policies and the British enforcement of the Townshend Acts, which taxed tea, lead, paper, oil, and other materials. These disputes led to a scuffle at the shipyards of Boston between a British soldier and a group of colonists.

- British troops showed up to quiet the dispute and secure trade at the port, but the mob turned on the British troops who fired into the crowd, killing five colonists, including Crispus Attucks, a black dock worker.

- The event was portrayed by the likes of Paul Revere as an example of British tyranny.

Link it Back

Disputes over trade, taxes, and repressive policies turned Boston into a hotbed of tension between the colonists and the British.

Link it Forward

The massacre became a unifying event for many colonists outside of Boston who were previously unaffected by British policies in the early 1770s.

THE BOSTON MASSACRE: 1770

The Boston Tea Party: 1773

- In 1773, the British passed the Tea Act which allowed British tea to be sold in the Colonies virtually free of taxation, while the colonial merchants paid a fee to the British government. The Tea Act was passed by Parliament in an attempt to save the struggling British East India Company from economic trouble. This unfair policy set off the Tea Party.

- Samuel Adams and other Bostonians urged the Massachusetts governor to send back a shipment of 500,000 pounds of British tea, but the Colonial government waffled, so the colonists took action.

- The colonial group, the Sons of Liberty, disguised themselves as Native Americans and dumped 18,000 pounds of tea into Boston Harbor to protest the Tea Act, as well as British tax policies which hurt colonists and colonial businesses. This act of economic terrorism was intended to get the attention of the British government living in the colonies as well as British government officials in England.

Link it Back

The Tea Act was part of a long line of oppressive taxes the British used to pay for their military presence, which enraged many colonists. The Tea Act/Tea Party situation was another example of a continuous cycle of oppressive British policies which led to colonial rebellions.

Link it Forward

The Tea Party foreshadowed the aggressive actions that would be undertaken by colonists during the pending revolution.

THE BOSTON TEA PARTY: 1773

The Intolerable Acts: 1774

- The British passed a series of oppressive laws, called the Coercive Acts, which were in response to the Boston Tea Party and other smaller acts of colonial rebellion.

- Colonists named these laws the Intolerable Acts. The acts called for repayment of the tea lost in the Tea Party as well as other punishments for colonists, including:

    ✓ Passing the Quartering Act, which allowed British troops to seize colonial properties.

    ✓ Closing the Boston Harbor.

    ✓ Declaring martial law in Boston.

    ✓ Raising taxes on a variety of goods.

    ✓ Dissolving the Massachusetts legislature—to imply that all colonies could receive a similar fate.

Link it Back

Following the Boston Massacre, the British government and colonial leaders viewed each other with much suspicion. The momentum caused by the Tea Party made the British government strengthen their hold upon the colonists.

Link it Forward

The Intolerable Acts pushed the colonists to create the Declaration of Colonial Rights, which outlined complaints about the British. It stated that the colonists would match force with force if the British used military aggression.

THE INTOLERABLE ACTS: 1774

The Battles of Lexington and Concord: 1775

- Paul Revere and others spread the word that 700 British regulars were marching on Concord, MA, from Boston to check on an arsenal which was thought to have a stockpile of weapons amassed by the colonists. Roughly 65 to 70 Minutemen (colonial militia members) met them a few miles down the road in Lexington, MA. After a brief skirmish in Lexington, eight Minutemen lay dead.

- The British arrived in Concord to a recently emptied arsenal and attempted to return to Boston, but they were met by more than 3,500 Minutemen who killed as many as 80 British soldiers before British reinforcements arrived.

- These battles proved to be a major morale boost for a militia which was previously considered no match against the powerful British military. These events are often called the "shot heard 'round the world" because the success of the colonists spurred revolutions all over the world.

Link it Back

The stockpiling of weapons was a result of the First Continental Congress's vow to retaliate if the British moved aggressively upon the colonists.

Link it Forward

Thomas Paine wrote his famous pamphlet, *Common Sense*, only after being motivated by the stories of the courage of colonists at the battles of Lexington and Concord.

The Battles of Lexington and Concord: 1775

Common Sense: 1776

- *Common Sense* is a 50-page pamphlet written by Thomas Paine. It used simplified language, biblical references, and a reasonable claim that colonists would never enjoy true political, social, and economic freedom under British rule.

- It was particularly successful in unifying colonists from a broad range of backgrounds.

Link it Back

Prior to the end of the French and Indian War, the British employed salutary neglect, a policy that relaxed the enforcement of British Parliament's laws meant to keep the colonies obedient. The end of the war meant the initiation of higher taxes. This led the British to tighten control over their subjects.

Link it Forward

When asked what motivated them to fight against the powerful British Army, many Continental soldiers cited the clear explanation of British oppression they received from Paine's pamphlet. Even George Washington credited Paine with motivating all colonists.

Common Sense: 1776

The Declaration of Independence: 1776

- In the summer of 1776, leaders of the Second Continental Congress asked individual colonies to form their own "state" governments while they began preparation for a formal Declaration of Independence from British rule.

- Thomas Jefferson drafted a document based on the ideas of Enlightenment Era philosophers. He used language which:

    ✓ Argued that all men are entitled to certain unalienable rights, which include "Life, Liberty, and the Pursuit of Happiness."

    ✓ Stated that "All men are created equal."

    ✓ Outlined the many grievances of the colonies, including taxation without representation, an unfair system of justice, and a glaring lack of civil liberties.

- The document also served as a declaration of war with the British, who would not allow this push toward self-governance in one of their colonial holdings.

Link it Back

For years, disputes over basic freedoms, tax policies, and unjust laws were building toward the colonist's declaration for independence. By 1776, the colonists and the British had very different views regarding the future of their relationship.

Link it Forward

The claim that "all men are created equal" caught the attention of Native Americans, free Blacks, and women, who argued that America claimed to be a land of liberty, but did little to show those groups the fruits of that freedom.

THE DECLARATION OF INDEPENDENCE: 1776

The British Surrender at Yorktown: 1781

- French and colonial forces moved on British General Charles Cornwallis at Yorktown, Virginia, while French naval reinforcements defeated a British fleet and then blocked all British entrance to the Chesapeake Bay.

- With no place to retreat, and no chance of support from British naval reinforcements, Cornwallis's aide surrendered to General Washington and the Marquis de Lafayette of France in October of 1781.

- Following the surrender, the Treaty of Paris was signed in 1783, which granted America its independence. It also set the geographic boundaries of the new nation, from Canada in the North to the Florida border in the South, to the Mississippi River in the West.

Link it Back

Benjamin Franklin traveled to Paris in 1778 to negotiate an alliance between France and the colonists. France recognized America as an independent nation and sought a trade agreement to benefit both nations.

Link it Forward

When US General John Pershing and his men landed in France to aid the French in WWI, his personal aide, Colonel Charles E. Stanton, stated, "Lafayette, we are here!" This was a simple thank you to France for their role in our revolution.

The British Surrender at Yorktown: 1781

"Those French are great fighters... how will we ever repay them?"

Chapter 2

Chapter 2:

American Government –

We Make a Rough Draft and Leave Some Room for Editing

Examples of American Democracy

- Following the end of the war, the Founding Fathers sought examples of effective and functional democratic institutions that were being used by various colonial governments of the time.

- The Virginia House of Burgesses was the first popularly elected legislature in the New World. The legislature consisted of representatives from all 11 of Virginia's districts. The House of Burgesses passed colonial laws and raised taxes that could be vetoed by an English governor. The US Congress was derived from these foundations.

- New England Town Hall Meetings were first used in 1633 in Massachusetts. The meetings were an example of direct democracy in small New England communities where citizens met, debated, and voted on laws as individuals. The emphasis on debate and rhetoric was popular among the Founding Fathers.

Link it Back

Many of the Founding Fathers, such as Richard Henry Lee, Patrick Henry, and George Washington, served in the House of Burgesses where they experienced the benefits of representative democracy.

Link it Forward

Suffrage (voting) in the Burgesses in Virginia was heavily restricted during the Colonial era, but as independence from England was achieved, voting was gradually expanded to include more Americans.

EXAMPLES OF AMERICAN DEMOCRACY

The Weaknesses of the Articles of Confederation: 1781

- The Second Continental Congress created a plan for government that favored an alliance of the 13 states. The framers of the Articles of Confederation chose to have a plan that stressed powerful and independent state governments over that of a strong central government.

- The new states favored this idea because many had operated as independent colonies when they were under British rule. A strong central authority was feared to be too much like a monarch.

- The articles had some weaknesses. They did not make provisions for:

    ✓ A strong central government.

    ✓ A common currency among the states.

    ✓ A president.

    ✓ Federal courts.

    ✓ A powerful federal military.

- The Articles of Confederation were passed in 1781. They lasted until the US Constitution replaced them in 1789.

Link it Back

Many of the early founders believed that a republic with a strong centralized government could never function in America simply because of its size and widespread populace. Travel and communication were very difficult at the time.

Link it Forward

The authors of the Articles of Confederation struggled to preserve states' rights, slavery, and fugitive slave laws to protect slave owners. These same debates on states' rights and slavery would ignite the Civil War in 1861.

THE WEAKNESSES OF THE ARTICLES OF CONFEDERATION: 1781

Northwest Ordinance: 1787

- The Northwest Ordinance was one of the few bright spots under the Articles of Confederation. It established that the Northwest Territory would be divided into no fewer than three and no more than five states.

- More importantly, it established a process for adding states to the Union.

- The Northwest Ordinance also deemed slavery to be illegal in any territory or state created in that part of the United States.

Link it Back

The Land Ordinance of 1785 preceded the Northwest Ordinance. It allowed sections of land in the West to be sold to the public for no less than one dollar per acre with a maximum of 640 acres per buyer. Many members of Congress saw this as a fundraising effort of a poor nation.

Link it Forward

In order to encourage the settlement of land in the Northwest Territory (and beyond), Congress passed the Homestead Act of 1862. This act granted 160 acres of land, free-of-charge, to those who chose to live in the western portion of the country for at least five years.

NORTHWEST ORDINANCE : 1787

Shays' Rebellion: 1786 - 1787

- Daniel Shays was a highly decorated soldier of the Continental Army during the Revolutionary War. A farmer from western Massachusetts, Shays' time in the military meant his farm went untended, and he fell on hard times.

- Those hard times did not stop state tax collection. Boston bankers also continued to demand the money they were owed from Shays and other farmers who owed mortgage payments. Many who could not pay were placed in debtors' prison. Shays led protests against these practices. What started out as spontaneous protests of farmers turned into an organized movement to attack state officials and bank operators in Boston.

- When the state of Massachusetts asked for federal help in ending the uprising, it became evident that the federal government was under funded and powerless to intervene in a state issue because of the restrictions of the Articles of Confederation.

- Shays and a group of 1,200 of his followers moved on an arsenal of weapons in Springfield, MA, but they were halted by a group of well-armed state militia men. Some of Shays' men were punished while Shays was released for fear that his imprisonment might spark another uprising. This rebellion reflected the need of the young nation to have a central government to provide oversight and support for individual states and their citizens.

Link it Back

Daniel Shays received the sword of the Marquis de Lafayette of France during the Revolutionary War for his bravery and courage. This was a major honor, but Shays had to sell the sword to help support his struggling farm.

Link it Forward

George Washington took notice of the uprising in Massachusetts and came out of political retirement to call for a convention to revise the Articles of Confederation in order to strengthen the federal government. The Constitutional Convention was assembled five months later.

SHAYS' REBELLION: 1786-1787

The Constitutional Convention: 1787

- Upon meeting in Philadelphia in May of 1787, it took less than a week for the members of the Constitutional Convention to realize that the Articles of Confederation were beyond revision and repair. Their focus would now be to create a federal government that could function without becoming too powerful.

- The opening sessions of the Constitutional Convention were not attended by major figures, such as Richard Henry Lee, Patrick Henry, Thomas Jefferson, John Adams, Samuel Adams, and John Hancock, because none of them believed that significant change would happen so quickly.

- The US Constitution, and its major systems, would not be ratified until 1789.

Link it Back

Shays' Rebellion was the largest of several citizen revolts that drew the attention of George Washington and resulted in his call for the Constitutional Convention. Smaller rebellions, from Georgia to New Hampshire, caught the attention of state officials who were concerned about full-scale revolutions beginning in their states.

Link it Forward

Americans were concerned that the authority of the federal government would resemble the tyranny of the British King. To quell this fear, the US Constitution created the federal system of government, which defined the powers held or shared by states and the federal government, and created a separation of power.

THE CONSTITUTIONAL CONVENTION: 1787

Federalists v. Anti-Federalists: 1787 - 1789

- National leaders debated the proper structure for the US government. Some of the most vocal Federalists (supporters of the Constitution) and Anti-Federalists (opponents of the Constitution) worked to clarify their position and win support for ratifying or rejecting the Constitution.

- Federalists worked to ratify the new Constitution. They supported:
    - ✓ A strong central government.
    - ✓ A limit on state powers.
    - ✓ A large republic.
    - ✓ An economy which relied on a growing industry.
    - ✓ A strong merchant class.

- Federalists were concerned that a bill of rights would allow the government ONLY to enforce the specific stated rights listed, as opposed to providing basic rights and civil liberties.

- Anti-Federalists opposed the passing of the new Constitution. They supported:
    - ✓ A government of loosely organized states.
    - ✓ An amended Articles of Confederation.
    - ✓ An economy which relied upon small family farms and craftspeople.
    - ✓ A preservation of slavery in states where it already existed.

- Anti-Federalists demanded a bill of rights be added to the Constitution to limit the power of the federal government, and to ensure personal freedoms.

- John Jay, James Madison, and Alexander Hamilton wrote essays, known as the *Federalist Papers*, that urged the passing of the Constitution, which had been crafted at the Philadelphia Convention. The *Anti-Federalist Papers* were similar essays that made the case for an amended Articles of Confederation. Both sides were aware that it would take 9 out of the 13 colonies to affirm the Constitution for it to be officially ratified.

Link it Back

The Articles of Confederation were a reflection of America's need to move away from the strong centralized authority of the British crown. Many of the colonial leaders felt that states were already well prepared to govern themselves independently.

Link it Forward

On June 21, 1788, New Hampshire became the ninth state to affirm the Constitution, ensuring the ratification (or passing) of the Constitution.

Federalists v. Anti-Federalists: 1787-1789

The Great Compromise: 1787

- The first major task of the Constitutional Conventional was to create a new legislative branch. Virginia, led by Governor Edmund J. Randolph and James Madison, called for a plan which created a two-house (bicameral) legislature with both houses receiving representation based on the population of individual states. Large states supported this plan, which was referred to as the Virginia Plan.

- A second option, the New Jersey Plan, was put forth by William Patterson. This plan called for a one house legislature that provided equal representation for all states regardless of population. This plan was supported by smaller states not wishing to be diminished by the authority of larger states.

- Roger Sherman of Connecticut suggested a plan that called for a bicameral legislature in which one house has representation by population (House of Representatives) and a second house with equal representation (Senate). The Great Compromise is sometimes called the "Connecticut Compromise." This plan established the US Congress we know today.

Link it Back

During the English occupation of the colonies, Virginia established itself as a powerful colonial government because of its population and economic prosperity. Virginians, such as Edmund J. Randolph and James Madison, had influential voices during the Constitutional Convention.

Link it Forward

The Great Compromise served notice to skeptical states' rights advocates that there was an air of compromise and healthy debate in the new republic. This flexibility would help to get the Constitution ratified in 1789.

THE GREAT COMPROMISE: 1787

3/5 Compromise: 1787

- Based on the Great Compromise, states' representation in the House of Representatives was to be based on the population of the individual state. The members of the Constitutional Convention were left to decide which people within the states were counted on the state census (count of state residents).

- Southern states wanted to count all Blacks in order to increase their representation, to remain relevant in the law-making process, and to ensure that their specific issues (e.g., slavery, tariff reform, states' rights, etc.) were addressed at the federal level.

- Opponents of slavery sought to exclude Blacks from all the state censuses because, at the time, Blacks were not granted citizenship under US laws. That plan would lessen the influence of southern slave states.

- The compromise allowed states to count five Blacks as being equal to three Whites in terms of deciding state representation. This was a major victory for slave owners who used the threat of rejecting the Constitution as leverage in brokering this deal.

- The 3/5 Compromise represents a stain on the history of our nation. Intended or not, the deal made the life of a black person worth 60% of a white citizen.

Link it Back

The Northwest Ordinance of 1787 outlawed slavery in any territories or states which were created within the Northwest Territory.

Link it Forward

Eli Whitney patented the cotton gin in 1794. It sped up the rate of seed removal from cotton and allowed manufacturers to process more cotton for textiles. The invention also amplified the need for slaves in the South due to the increased demand for raw cotton. From 1794 to 1820, the US imported as many slaves as there were in America during the entire colonial period.

3/5 COMPROMISE: 1787

Preamble / Powers of the Three Branches

- The opening statement of the Constitution (called the Preamble) was written by Governor Morris of Virginia in order to outline the goals of the US Constitution and provide a list of informal promises to the American people.

- These promises include:
    - ✓ Establishing justice (e.g., court systems).
    - ✓ Ensuring domestic tranquility (e.g., law enforcement).
    - ✓ Providing for the common defense (e.g., military branches).
    - ✓ Promoting the general welfare (e.g., social security).
    - ✓ Securing the blessings of liberty (e.g., voter protection).

Article I: Legislative Branch

Congress: declares war, coins money, creates an army and navy, regulates commerce, establishes rules of immigration and naturalization, and establishes federal courts.

Article II: Executive Branch

The President: vetoes or signs bills as chief legislator, controls the military as commander-in-chief, acts as the head law enforcer as chief executive, and deals with world leaders as chief diplomat.

Article III: Judicial Branch

The Supreme Court: upholds laws and executive actions as constitutional or declares them unconstitutional (judicial review). Constitutional historians debate whether or not the Founding Fathers intended for the court to have judicial review, but the case of *Marbury v. Madison* (1803) solidified their authority as legal.

Link it Back

In the original wording of the Constitution, the president was elected by the Electoral College; the Senate was appointed by state legislatures; and federal judges were appointed by the president. The House of Representatives, therefore, was the only group in government elected by a purely democratic electorate. For that reason, the House of Representatives has been aptly nicknamed, "The People's House."

Link it Forward

The president also acts as chief (head) of state. This is an informal role for the president who is charged with comforting, motivating, and sometimes, scolding the American public. The president might cut a ribbon to open a national park, throw out the first pitch at the World Series, attend the funeral of a world leader, or publicly address the nation to ease fears.

PREAMBLE / POWERS OF THE THREE BRANCHES

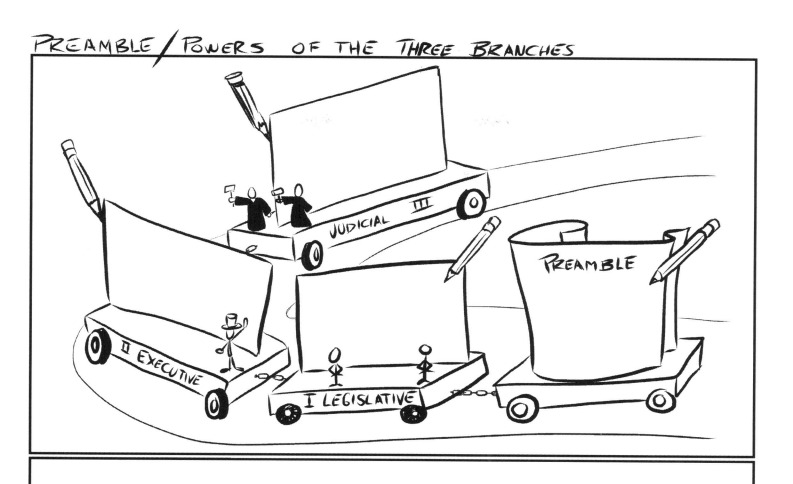

Federalism (The Federal System)

- The Constitution created a federal system of government which split power between the federal (national) government and state governments, with the two sharing some powers. The language of the Constitution made it clear that the federal government retained supreme power.

  - ✓ Key federal (delegated) powers: coining money, maintaining a military, and conducting foreign affairs

  - ✓ Key state (reserved) powers: maintaining roads, conducting elections, and maintaining schools

  - ✓ Key shared (concurrent) powers: collecting taxes and setting up courts

Link it Back

The federal system is loosely based on the ancient Roman Republic system which created provincial and local governments in order to help organize the massive Roman Empire. This allowed local governments within the provinces to serve the needs of specific areas, while leaders in Rome retained supreme authority.

Link it Forward

Federal authority was challenged at Little Rock High School in 1957. Arkansas Governor Orville Faubus defied a federal order to proceed with school integration. President Dwight D. Eisenhower ordered US Army troops to enforce the integration mandate and ensure the safety of nine black students enrolled at the school.

Federalism (The Federal System)

Checks and Balances

- The separation of powers divides government into three branches, each with separate powers. The legislative branch (Congress) creates laws, the executive branch (President) enforces laws, and the judicial branch (Courts) interprets laws.

- Though the branches are separated, they constantly work together to ensure that laws in the US meet the needs of the American people.

- Checks and balances were created as a means of making sure that the federal government did not allow one branch to gain too much power and dominate government. Most founders were worried that a strong president could start to act as a monarch unless their powers were held in check.

- Big checks:

    ✓ <u>Legislative</u>—Congress can use a 2/3 vote to override an executive veto and impeach executive and judicial officials, and the Senate (not the House) must approve judges appointed by the president, as well as presidential treaties.

    ✓ <u>Executive</u>—The president can veto or sign bills approved by Congress, and the president must appoint federal judges to their posts. The president can co-sponsor legislation and often uses the "bully pulpit" (the president's far-reaching media presence) to influence bills. The president also pardons (forgives) convicted and suspected criminals.

    ✓ <u>Judicial</u>—Justices receive a lifetime appointment. Federal courts can use the power of judicial review to declare executive orders and congressionally-approved laws unconstitutional.

Link it Back

French philosopher Baron de Montesquieu created the theory of separation of powers. In Book XI, chapter VI of *The Spirit of the Laws*, he said, "When the legislative and executive powers are united in the same person, or in the same body of magistrates, there can be no liberty."

Link it Forward

President Franklin D. Roosevelt attempted to alter the system of checks and balances by adding six justices to the Supreme Court, which was declaring some of his New Deal programs unconstitutional. This "court packing" was rejected by Congress because it gave too much authority to the executive branch.

CHECKS AND BALANCES

Unwritten Constitution

- "Unwritten constitution" is a term used to describe ideas and practices of the US government that have become entrenched in their traditions and day-to-day work. These traditions and practices are not actually part of the original Constitution or any of the first ten amendments. The groups and systems are effective, so they have become accepted as part of our government.

- Some of the best examples of the unwritten constitution include:

    ✓ The President's Cabinet: the president's main advisors.

    ✓ Committees in Congress: groups of Congresspersons who review and vote on bills prior to there presentation on the floor of the House or Senate. This is done to speed up the work of law making.

    ✓ Political Parties: groups of politicians and voters who share common beliefs and priorities.

Link it Back

The House of Representatives created the first standing committee in 1789 to address the slow process of reviewing enrolled bills. The US Senate did not create any permanent committees until 1816.

Link it Forward

George Washington's original cabinet included four posts: attorney general, secretary of state, secretary of the treasury, and secretary of war. Contemporary presidents have a cabinet comprised of the heads of all fifteen executive departments, as well as a national security team.

UNWRITTEN CONSTITUTION

UNWRITTEN CONSTITUTION

The Bill of Rights: 1791

- The Bill of Rights refers to the first ten amendments of the US Constitution, which include provisions for freedoms such as speech, press, religion, privacy, and the right to bear arms. The amendments also include protections such as due process of law, protection against illegal search and seizure, protection against cruel and unusual punishments, and the right to have an attorney and a trial by jury.

- The Bill of Rights is meant to protect citizens from the powers of their own government and to generally limit the power of the government.

Link it Back

The Bill of Rights was added to the Constitution as part of a "handshake" agreement between federalists and anti-federalists who wanted an assurance that the power of the federal government would not infringe upon the individual liberties of American citizens.

Link it Forward

Almost no aspect of American democracy is as hotly contested and debated as the First Amendment guarantee of free speech. In the 1989 case of *Texas v. Johnson*, Johnson was convicted of "desecration of a venerated object" when he burned an American flag to protest the policies of President Ronald Reagan. This conviction was overturned by a lower federal court and then upheld by the Supreme Court as symbolic speech.

THE BILL OF RIGHTS: 1791

Chapter 3

Chapter 3:

HATCHING THE POWER EAGLE

Jefferson's America v. Hamilton's America

- Thomas Jefferson, the secretary of state under President George Washington, envisioned an America consisting of farmers and simple craftspeople who participated in a government which had most of its power embedded at the state and local level. Jefferson distrusted a strong central government and an industrialized American economy because he believed that American freedom was rooted in the simplicity of an agricultural life.

- Alexander Hamilton, the secretary of treasury under President Washington, envisioned an America consisting of farming, but also of massive industrial centers, international trade, and a national bank to support industrialization, which aided the process of repaying war debt.

Link it Back

In the end, Hamilton's plan won out due to public concerns regarding our significant Revolutionary War debt, which amounted to millions of dollars. That overwhelming number swayed public opinion toward Hamilton's viewpoint.

Link it Forward

President Jefferson's plan of limiting the power of the federal government was tested by an offer from France to purchase the Louisiana Territory. The land held great promise for the nation, but the Constitution did not clearly spell out the federal government's role in land purchases. Jefferson made the deal by interpreting the Constitution as a flexible document and accepting that the federal government had vast authority.

The Whiskey Rebellion: 1794

- In 1791, Secretary of the Treasury Alexander Hamilton levied an excise (luxury) tax on whiskey sales. The excise taxes of 1791 were imposed in order to strengthen the nation's economic condition and to provide the federal government with an opportunity to show its supremacy over state and local governments.

- In 1794, angry whiskey distillers in western Pennsylvania protested the tax by attacking the home of a tax collector and other tax officials in the days that followed. Hamilton urged President Washington to use military force, but he instead called upon state militias to negotiate a settlement.

- State militia groups failed to reach an agreement, and President Washington sent 13,000 federal troops to end the rebellion. This was an early example of the federal government using military power to enforce a federal law or tax. This is federalism.

Link it Back

In 1765, colonists protested the British Parliament's Stamp Act by attacking tax collectors and refusing to pay the tax. After a lengthy debate in England, Parliament determined the tax to be unfair and it was repealed.

Link it Forward

In 1832, Andrew Jackson threatened to send troops to South Carolina in order to collect a federal tariff (tax on imported goods) that was nullified by the state's government. South Carolina eventually paid the tariff, which was lowered by the federal government. This nullification exemplified the growing debate between the interests of individual states and the supremacy of the federal government.

THE WHISKEY REBELLION: 1794

George Washington's Farewell Address (Essay): 1796

- George Washington's Farewell Address appeared in the *American Daily Advertiser*. In this address, Washington notified the American public that he would voluntarily relinquish his role as the nation's president in order to ensure that the office of the president changed hands regularly to make certain that it did not resemble a monarchy. Historians believe that much of this essay was authored by Secretary of the Treasury Alexander Hamilton.

- In his address, Washington foretold that:

    ✓ Political parties would divide the nation.

    ✓ Foreign alliances could draw the US into costly wars across the globe.

Link it Back

Shortly after the Revolutionary War, George Washington retired his commission as commander of the Continental Army. Chaotic events, such as Shays' Rebellion, would eventually draw Washington from retirement with the intention of creating a more stable federal government.

Link it Forward

Washington's warnings of divisive political parties were based on the actions of his own cabinet members. Thomas Jefferson, Washington's secretary of state, formed the Democratic-Republican Party, which worked for states' rights and personal liberties. They opposed the views of Alexander Hamilton, Washington's secretary of the treasury, and his Federalist Party, which supported a strong central presence in law-making and the economy.

George Washington's Farewell Address (Essay): 1796

John Adams — A Troubled Presidency 1797 - 1801

- John Adams was forced to raise taxes in order to help pay for continued war debt, build the country's infrastructure, and ensure military preparedness. Whether the government needed the tax money or not, paying increased taxes was not popular with the American public, which was struggling to make ends meet.

- Adams also inherited a looming trade war with France due to concerns about the US-British agreement over the Northwest Territory and its possible violation of the France-US alliance.

- France had begun to impress (steal) US ships, and Adams sent a delegation to France to meet with French Foreign Minister Charles Maurice de Tallyrand to negotiate an end to the tension. The French government sent three men who came to be known as X, Y, and Z (who were political nobodies) to demand a bribe to see Tallyrand. This infuriated Adams, and the US waged an undeclared naval war against France. Adams regained some stature with the public, albeit for a short time.

- Adams continued to struggle with economic instability, and the opposing Democratic-Republican Party continued to condemn his actions. Many Democratic-Republicans were immigrants (aliens), and the criticism of the president was perceived by some of Adams' supporters as a threat against national security.

- In response Adams created the Alien and Sedition Acts. These acts made the process of gaining citizenship tougher for vocal immigrants of the Democratic-Republican Party, and the Sedition Acts punished all anti-government speech.

Link it Back

John Adams served as vice president to George Washington, and in many ways, the imposing shadow of Washington may have doomed Adams' presidency. European powers and states' rights advocates tested Adams' authority from the beginning of his presidency to determine if he could live up to the standards of his predecessor.

Link it Forward

The two main Democratic-Republicans, Thomas Jefferson and James Madison, took immediate action against the Alien and Sedition Acts. They pushed through resolutions in Kentucky and Virginia that called for states to nullify federal laws that were deemed unconstitutional. This resolution was used in 1832 by South Carolina, which felt that a federal tariff violated the US Constitution.

John Adams — A Troubled Presidency: 1797-1801

Louisiana Purchase: 1803

- Napoleon Bonaparte, a French ruler, offered to sell the Louisiana Territory to the US for the low price of $15 million. This meant that the US could potentially double in size, gain the port of New Orleans (the mouth of the Mississippi River), increase trade in the West, and do it all for pennies per acre.

- The trouble with the deal came from Jefferson's own views as a strict constructionist in regards to the principles of the Constitution, which means he held a literal view of our legal foundations. He doubted that the federal government had the authority to authorize the deal because land purchasing powers were not clearly spelled out in the Constitution.

- In the end, Jefferson stretched his views of the Constitution and made the deal with Napoleon. He saw the purchase as beneficial to the US economy, and felt that federal authority could be strengthened to meet the needs of American expansion and trade.

Link it Back

The Louisiana Territory was supposed to be a supplier of food and natural resources to the French Empire, but France was spending millions fighting the British and putting down rebellions. The land deal was simply made to pay off French debt.

Link it Forward

As Americans moved westward to settle in the Louisiana Territory, questions circled around the legality of slavery in the new territories and states created by the purchase.

Louisiana Purchase: 1803

The Lewis and Clark Expedition: 1804 - 1806

- Before the Louisiana Purchase was finalized, President Thomas Jefferson had begun the process of commissioning his personal secretary, Meriwether Lewis, to command an expeditionary force in the newly acquired land. Lewis selected William Clark to help lead a group of 45 men, known as the "Corps of Discovery," on a two-year journey.

- President Jefferson charged Lewis and Clark with:

    ✓ Creating maps of the territory.

    ✓ Trying to find both land and water routes westward.

    ✓ Providing detailed information about various tribes in the West.

    ✓ Strengthening America's claim to the disputed Oregon Territory by providing a strong presence in the area.

- When the Corps of Discovery reached present-day North Dakota, they were joined by a teenage mother named Sacagawea who was a member of the Shoshone tribe, which lived on land in the present-day Idaho region of the Rocky Mountains. Sacagawea proved to be invaluable with her knowledge of tribal languages, safe passageways through the mountains, and map making skills. She eventually brokered a deal with the Shoshones for horses, which aided the expeditionary force tremendously.

Link it Back

When the Jamestown Settlement was founded in 1607, Queen Elizabeth I of England agreed to provide partial funding for the expedition because she was promised that the Jamestown leadership would search for a water route to the Pacific.

Link it Forward

Months into their journey, Lewis and Clark realized that an unforeseen benefit of Sacagawea's presence was her infant son. It was well understood by many tribes that no warring party would consider bringing a baby with them to conquer land. The baby was a symbol that the corps came with peaceful intentions.

The Lewis and Clark Expedition: 1804-1806

Marbury v. Madison: 1803

- In the final hours of his presidency, John Adams appointed a series of "midnight judges." This term references the last minute appointment of these men by Adams. These appointments were carried out in order to strengthen the power of Adams' party (federalists). One of those appointments was William Marbury, who had received the necessary congressional approval to be awarded the job.

- Based on the Judiciary Act of 1789, new judges needed signed presidential authorization to take their seats, and new president, Thomas Jefferson, ordered his secretary of state, James Madison, to withhold the authorization.

- The case was reviewed by the Supreme Court because some congressional members argued that the president could not discontinue the appointment process because Marbury had already received congressional approval. The case went to the Supreme Court because it required a third party to decide which branch (executive or legislative) held authority in this decision.

- The court ruled that it was wrong for Madison to withhold authorization, but it also ruled that the Judiciary Act was unconstitutional. Marbury did not receive the post.

- Of greater importance in the Marbury case was the establishment of the principle of judicial review of federal laws, which strengthened the courts as well as the federal government's abilities to interpret state laws and review lower court rulings. Judicial review ensures that government policies, laws, executive orders, and court rulings are constitutional.

Link it Back

There were several state courts which undertook judicial review prior to 1803, but until the Marbury case, it was unclear if the US Supreme Court held that authority.

Link it Forward

This was the first of many cases in which the Supreme Court, led by Chief Justice John Marshall, expanded the power of the federal government.

MARBURY V. MADISON: 1803

McCulloch v. Maryland: 1819

- The Maryland legislature passed a law that placed a state tax on the Second National Bank of the United States, a federal bank set up by Congress and located in Maryland. The cashier of the federally controlled bank, James McCulloch, refused to pay the tax, and the Maryland courts ruled in favor of the state. McCulloch appealed the decision.

- The Supreme Court, led by Chief Justice John Marshall, first determined that Congress DID have the ability to set up a federal bank; then they cited the Supremacy Clause in order to determine that the federal bank DID NOT have to pay state taxes. (Federal laws and practices were superior to that of state laws and practices.)

- This ruling strengthened the power of the federal government over state governments.

Link it Back

The formation of a national bank has been controversial since the idea was introduced by Alexander Hamilton. Hamilton sought to help pay off war debt and create an economy that supports expanding businesses. Many states' rights advocates felt that a national bank gave the federal government too much influence over the direction of the economy.

Link it Forward

Many of the Marshall Court's decisions empowered the federal government, but they also made strong states' rights advocates in the South wary of federal expansion. They worried that an empowered federal government could potentially bring an end to slavery.

McCULLOCH V. MARYLAND : 1819

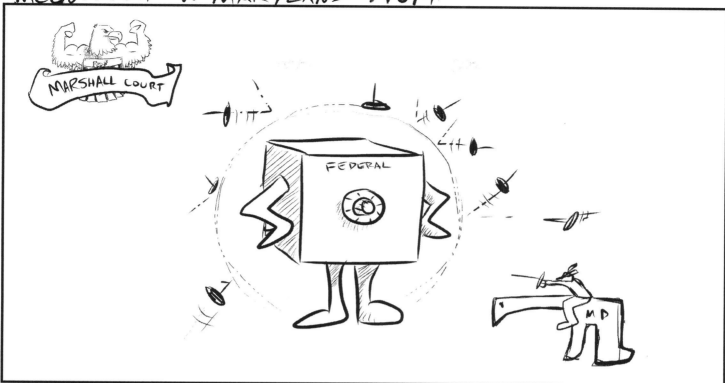

Gibbons v. Ogden: 1824

- Robert Fulton invented the steamboat, and in 1798, he received a 20 year state monopoly license from New York to operate steamboats in the state. Fulton's company assigned a man named Aaron Ogden the duty of operating a ferry service between New York and New Jersey.

- A man named Thomas Gibbons received a federal license to operate a competing New York-to-New Jersey ferry company, and Ogden obtained an injunction (court order) to keep Gibbons' boats from docking in NY, because it violated his state issued monopoly license. Gibbons appealed because he had a legal federal license to operate his business.

- The Supreme Court, led by John Marshall, argued that the Commerce Clause of Article 1, Section 8 of the Constitution gave Congress the ability to regulate trade between the US and foreign governments, but also gave Congress the power to regulate interstate trade to ensure that business can be conducted between states that may have varying laws regarding shipping and trade. The court ruled in favor of Gibbons and determined that Ogden's New York license was invalid because interstate trade falls under the jurisdiction of the federal government.

- This court ruling allowed the federal government to regulate interstate trade and expanded federal power even more.

Link it Back

Many historians argue that the main purposes of the Commerce Clause were to place restrictions on international trade, give protection to American merchants, and punish foreign traders who violate tariff laws or shipping codes.

Link it Forward

In 1887, Congress passed the Interstate Commerce Act, which created the Interstate Commerce Commission. It was designed to address the issues of railroad abuse and discrimination by creating the following rules: shipping rates had to be reasonable, rates had to be published, secret rebates were outlawed, and price discrimination was made illegal.

GIBBONS v. OGDEN: 1824

War of 1812

- By 1811, tension between the US and Great Britain was running high. The US accused the British of provoking Native American attacks in the Northwest Territory, interfering with trading and shipping routes, and impressing (stealing) American ships. British naval ships impressed US trade ships, kidnapped the sailors, and forced them to serve in the British Royal Navy.

- In 1812, President James Madison asked Congress to declare war on the British. This was NOT a clear cut decision for Congress. Some legislators in the Northeast believed that the war was being declared to serve the nation's need to expand westward, and coastal states in New England were sure that the war would disrupt shipping and trade. Many Americans felt the federal government should focus on the day-to-day financial concerns of average farmers and workers. War was declared, but Americans remained divided on the issue.

- The British found an ally in the Northwest Territory. Native Americans, including the famous Shawnee Chief Tecumseh, began to align tribes with the British to battle the Americans in order to prevent the westward expansion of American settlers into Native American territories.

- US troops attacked British installations in Canada and scored early victories. The British had later success against the Americans, but were thwarted when they tried to occupy major cities like Baltimore, MD. The British did seize control of Washington, DC, and burned down the White House.

- In 1814, the British and the Americans agreed to sign the Treaty of Ghent in Belgium. The treaty deemed that all conquered territories were to be returned, and there was a process in place to settle the boundaries between the US and Canada. The issues of impressment, westward expansion, and free trade were not discussed.

- Two weeks after the treaty was signed, Major-General Andrew Jackson, unaware of the peace plan because of how slowly information was communicated during the time, scored a major victory over British forces in New Orleans. The victory boosted US morale, but most historians agree that the war was a virtual draw.

Link it Back

Before the war ended, American poet Francis Scott Key penned the poem, "The Defence of Fort McHenry," after witnessing the bombardment of the fort in the Baltimore harbor. The poem was later turned into the "Star Spangled Banner." The song was officially named the American national anthem in 1931.

Link it Forward

In 1816, James Monroe's election ushered in the "Era of Good Feelings" in the US. The era was portrayed as a time of good relations between the US and European nations. In reality, it was the beginning of US isolationism, the era of compromise regarding slavery, and the onset of US industrialization.

War of 1812

Chapter 4

Chapter 4:

America Takes Some "Me" Time

Monroe Doctrine: 1823

- In 1823, President James Monroe created the Monroe Doctrine in which he stated that the Western Hemisphere (North, South, and Central America) was no longer open to colonization by European powers. In exchange, the United States would refrain from participation in European wars and would not disturb existing European colonies in the Western Hemisphere.

- The doctrine was created in response to the ongoing revolutions that were taking place in South and Central America, as well as the wars in Europe, which saw monarchs of major European nations each seeking to establish their authority across the continent. This was a bold foreign policy strategy, which gained marginal acceptance from Europeans who did not wish for the US to influence their conflicts. The Monroe Doctrine was a major milestone in a long period of US isolationism and industrial build up.

Link it Back

In his farewell address, George Washington warned of the US aligning itself with foreign powers because of the bloody consequences of major military conflicts.

Link it Forward

In the early 1900s, President Theodore Roosevelt extended the Monroe Doctrine to create the Roosevelt Corollary (Big Stick Policy) in which the US became a police presence in Central America to maintain order and economic progress in the Western Hemisphere.

MONROE DOCTRINE: 1823

Andrew Jackson and the Rise of Executive Power: 1829 - 1837

- Andrew Jackson's presidency represented a major turning point in the role of the executive branch. Jackson greatly expanded his role as president by repeatedly vetoing bills passed by both houses of Congress, expanding states' rights, and using his influence to expand slavery westward.

- Jackson fought against the use of protectionist tariffs (taxes on imports) because he felt they allowed businesses to raise prices that could hurt average consumers.

- Jackson also used his veto power to halt the re-chartering of the National Bank, which had been used to provide loans to big businesses and expand the industrialization of America. The veto represented strong support for common farmers and laborers who benefited little from the lending institution. Jackson is also considered to be the founder of the Democratic Party.

Link it Back
Jackson gained national popularity as a major-general in the War of 1812.

Link it Forward
Jackson is featured on the twenty dollar bill, which is ironic because he strongly opposed the re-chartering of a national bank.

Andrew Jackson and the Rise of Executive Power: 1829-1837

Andrew Jackson and the Spoils System

- Upon taking office in 1828, Jackson argued that he had the right to remove officials who had been hired or appointed by former presidents. Some of the officials had been there since the Washington Administration. He viewed many of these men as corrupt or complacent in their roles. He believed that every new president had the right to choose those in the executive branch who could help a president guide the country.

- Many of the people Jackson planned on hiring had been promised government jobs if he was elected, so they aided his election campaign. Jackson referred to this as "rotation in office," but when Senator William Marcy proclaimed, "To the victor belong the spoils" (benefits), Jackson's adversaries called it the "spoils system."

Link it Back

Jackson fought to hire his own people, but he relied heavily on unofficial advisors to run his campaign and presidency. These newspaper editors and old friends were dubbed the "kitchen cabinet."

Link it Forward

In 2013, the executive branch of government employed more than 4 million men and women.

ANDREW JACKSON AND THE SPOILS SYSTEM

Andrew Jackson and the Nullification Crisis: 1832

- In 1828, President John Quincy Adams signed what southerners referred to as the "Tariff of Abominations." This tariff placed an import tax on textiles and manufactured items because northern industries were being hurt by the artificially low prices on goods coming from Great Britain. Great Britain, in turn, sought other places for cotton purchases, and the tariff gravely threatened the southern economy.

- The South viewed this as clear favoritism toward northern states, which had much more manufacturing than the South. The South also saw this as a possible first step in the elimination of slavery because it infringed upon states' rights. For that reason, South Carolina nullified (chose not to pay) the tariff because it was harmful to the state economy. South Carolina, led by Vice President John Calhoun, threatened secession if the federal government intervened.

- Though Jackson was a major proponent of states' rights, he had to enforce the tariff in order to maintain the authority of the federal government. (This is federalism.) Jackson threatened military intervention if South Carolina continued its nullification policy. South Carolina backed down. It was agreed by all sides that a lowered tariff would be a fair compromise. This represented a strong show of power for the federal government, but it was also a precursor to a bigger issue involving states' rights and federal authority (the Civil War).

Link it Back

When Jackson campaigned against John Quincy Adams, he spoke out against tariffs, such as the "Tariff of Abominations," because he believed that tariffs raised overall prices for common people.

Link it Forward

South Carolina's threat to secede became real in 1860 following the election of Abraham Lincoln.

Andrew Jackson and the Nullification Crisis: 1832

Indian Removal Act and the Trail of Tears: 1830 - 1831

- As an army general, Andrew Jackson fought a number of wars against Native American tribes, with thousands of acres being seized from tribal governments. As president, Jackson signed the Indian Removal Act of 1830, which allowed the federal government to negotiate a "land-swap" with Native American tribes. The tribes were relocated to land in present-day Oklahoma. This act was a response to the influence of southern plantation owners who were seeking to seize valuable tribal lands on which they would grow cotton.

- Court rulings and treaties signed by the US government and Native American tribes stipulated that the land swap should be voluntary, but Jackson and the southern state governments ignored these rulings and policies, and used military force to remove the tribes. Native American properties were formerly protected by the federal government from state governments who sought to seize the land.

- By 1831, Jackson ordered the US Army to forcibly remove the Choctaw tribe from their land. The Creek and Cherokee tribes were removed soon after, losing 8,000 and 6,000 members respectively during their journeys westward. With no supplies, food, or assistance, one reporter called this trip a "trail of tears and death."

Link it Back

Andrew Jackson had no love for Native Americans. When questioned about his policies, he reminded Americans that Native Americans had sided against the US in the French and Indian War, the Revolutionary War, and the War of 1812.

Link it Forward

Though Native Americans were promised that their new land would be untouched by Whites, Oklahoma was made a state in 1907, and the native lands were reduced to small plots of federally-protected territory.

Indian Removal Act and the Trail of Tears: 1830-1831

The Alamo and the Mexican-American War: 1836 - 1848

- In the early 1820s, Americans settled in the Northern Mexican territory of Texas. This was allowed by the Mexican government to promote trade. As the migration of Americans continued, ownership of the territory was disputed between the Texans (American settlers) and the Mexican government. The Alamo, a church mission located in present-day San Antonio, became important in this struggle. The side in control of the Alamo seemed to be the side ruling Texas.

- In 1836, with roughly 200 Texans occupying the Alamo, a large Mexican force attacked the Alamo, killing nearly everyone in the mission. Months later, an army of Texans, led by General Sam Houston, defeated the Mexican force and sealed independence for Texas when Mexican General Santa Anna signed over the territory in order to spare his own life.

- Texas was given statehood in 1845, and in 1846, President James Polk instigated a war with Mexico who refused to sell the US lands that lay west of the Louisiana Territory. The Mexican-American war lasted two years with the US claiming victory. The US gave Mexico $15 million for all or parts of present-day California, Nevada, Utah, Arizona, Wyoming, Colorado, and New Mexico.

Link it Back

The US supported Mexico's independence movement against Spain from 1820-1821. The US supplied Mexican rebels with weapons and provided some soldiers with training in guerrilla warfare tactics.

Link it Forward

After the former Mexican territories were annexed, the slave debate became more delicate. Under Mexican law, slavery was illegal. Many abolitionist legislators argued that this land should remain free of slavery, no matter what compromises were put in place.

The Alamo and the Mexican-American War: 1836-1848

Seneca Falls Convention: 1848

- In 1848, abolitionists and women's rights activists Lucretia Mott and Elizabeth Cady Stanton organized the Seneca Falls Convention in Upstate New York. Mott and Stanton advertised the convention in Frederick Douglas's newspaper, *The North Star,* as "a convention to discuss the social, civil, and religious condition and rights of women." It was the first women's convention of its kind.

- Stanton introduced a Declaration of Sentiments and Grievances, which was a document that detailed the grave injustices perpetrated upon married women by their husbands. The document was closely modeled after the Declaration of Independence.

- On day two of the convention, men such as Frederick Douglass were invited to attend. There were twelve resolutions adopted at the convention, all dealing with equal treatment for women. One addressed the need for women to have the right to vote in order to become fully enfranchised into the US political system.

Link it Back

The Declaration of Independence lists its grievances by starting off sentences with "He will…" to illustrate the injustices carried out by the King of England. The Declaration of Sentiments and Grievances lists its grievances by starting off the sentences with "He has…" in order to show the control husbands had over their wives.

Link it Forward

Women did not receive the right to vote until the 19th Amendment was enacted more than seventy years later, in 1920.

Seneca Falls Convention: 1848

Susan B. Anthony

- Susan B. Anthony began her career speaking out against the evils of alcohol, but realized that her voice would never truly be heard until she had the right to vote. In 1869, along with Elizabeth Cady Stanton, she created the National Women's Suffrage Association (later called NAWSA). She also helped create the suffrage newspaper, *The Revolution*.

- Anthony gave many moving speeches that argued for women's suffrage, and she even voted in the 1872 presidential election…illegally. She received a fine of $100, which she never paid. Anthony petitioned government officials for the vote, but did not live long enough to see her efforts pay off. She died in 1906.

Link it Back

Like many women of the era, Anthony grew up supporting the abolitionist movement, which fought against slavery. Many female abolitionists later became active in the first women's rights movement.

Link it Forward

In 1979, the US Mint introduced the Susan B. Anthony dollar to honor Anthony's activism and legacy.

Susan B. Anthony

Dorothea Dix

- Dorothea Dix gained notoriety as an aggressive reformer of prisons and institutions for the mentally ill. In 1841, she began documenting the inhumane treatment of Massachusetts prisoners who were beaten, starved, and neglected. Many of these prisoners were incarcerated not for crimes, but because they were mentally ill. Dix pushed the state to provide separate facilities for the mentally ill so they could receive proper care. This was called the Asylum Movement.

- Dix's work eventually led to new treatments for the mentally ill, and her ideas spread to Western Europe, where the treatment of prisoners and patients was as deplorable as it was in the US.

Link it Back

Dix's father suffered from severe depression and struggled with alcoholism. She attributed her passion for helping the mentally ill to her experiences with her father's suffering.

Link it Forward

In 1963, John F. Kennedy signed the Community Mental Health Centers Act, which provided $150 million for the building of new mental health care facilities.

Dorothea Dix

Horace Mann

- Horace Mann is the father of the American public education system. In the early to mid-1800s, Mann became a major proponent of the idea that an education provided a foundation for the future of American democracy and for economic prosperity. Mann believed that education:

    ✓ Was the only way of teaching American children about the benefits of freedom.

    ✓ Should be free to all students.

    ✓ Should be provided to students of diverse ethnic, racial, and socio-economic backgrounds.

    ✓ Should be delivered by professionally licensed teachers.

Link it Back

Mann was in the Massachusetts House of Representatives where he worked to build better roads, bridges, and government buildings. It was here that he learned that education was the true foundation on which to build a stronger America.

Link it Forward

In 2011, there were roughly 3.3 million licensed teachers working in public schools in the US.

HORACE MANN

Chapter 5

Chapter 5:

KINDA ANGRY ABOUT SLAVERY TO

Super Duper Angry About Slavery

Sectionalism

- By the early-mid 1800s, it had become clear that the United States was divided into regions (sections), all of which had differing economic and social priorities.

<u>In the North</u> there was an emphasis on family farms, industrialization, and the wealth that ensued from these systems.

- In order to support industry, northern states endorsed a national bank, which provided loans to big businesses and federal tariffs (taxes on imported goods), which made American manufactured goods more attractive to buyers, while raising revenue.

- The North supported a strong federal government.

<u>In the South</u> there was an emphasis on an agricultural economy that featured the production of cash crops, such as cotton and tobacco, on plantations.

- The South opposed the National Bank, which they felt only supported northern industry and gave federal officials too much control over regional economies.

- Many southern states also opposed tariffs, which hindered their ability to buy inexpensive British imports, and also forced the British to place taxes on their cotton exports.

- The South fought for slavery and the rights of individual states to decide the slave issue, as opposed to the federal government controlling the fate of agriculturally dependent southern states.

<u>In the West</u> the main concern was settling western lands gained from the Louisiana Purchase, the Mexican Cession, the Oregon Treaty, and others.

- Western settlers needed US military support in their battles with Native Americans, and they soon needed railroad transportation to speed up trade.

Link it Back

Alexander Hamilton fought for the National Bank as a way to promote industry and foreign trade, which would help the US pay back millions in debt owed from the Revolutionary War.

Link it Forward

To encourage settlements out west, the federal government passed the Homestead Act, which offered Americans 160 acres of land if they settled upon it for at least five years.

SECTIONALISM

105

Missouri Compromise: 1820

- In the early 1800s, there was much concern in southern slave states about the federal government placing a ban on slavery, which would likely cripple the South's agricultural economy due to its reliance on slave labor. For that reason, as states were being admitted into the union, some lawmakers tried to keep the number of free and slave states equal, so that the votes in the US Senate were also equal. The House of Representatives was already controlled by the populous northern states.

- When the question of Missouri's statehood arose in 1820, lawmakers created a compromise that made Missouri a slave state; Maine (formerly controlled by Massachusetts), became a free state. From that point on, all land in the Louisiana Territory above the latitude line of 36', 30" was to be free of slavery. Slavery was preserved…but limited.

Link it Back

For many southerners, the slave issue was simply a states' rights debate. Most southern slave owners believed that the individual states in their section of the country, which relied upon slavery to generate wealth, should decide slave issues.

Link it Forward

This was the first major compromise of the "Era of Compromise" which slowly led the US toward the Civil War.

MISSOURI COMPROMISE: 1820

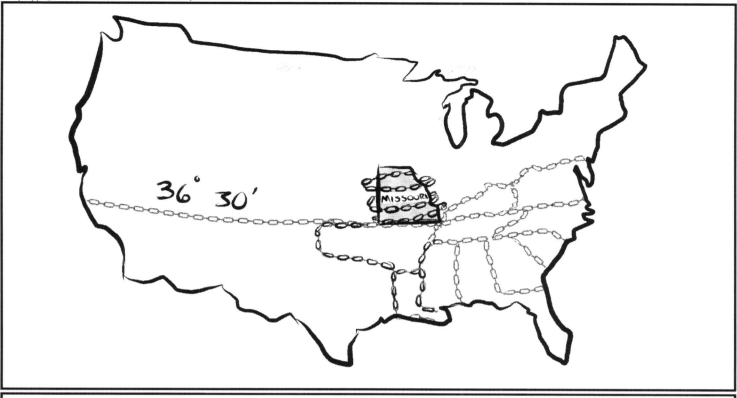

Nat Turner's Slave Rebellion: 1831

- In August of 1831, Virginia slave and preacher Nat Turner led a slave rebellion that killed roughly 60 white men, women, and children. Turner believed that he could communicate directly with God, and that God commanded him to kill his oppressors with their own weapons. Turner hid out for six weeks after the rebellion, but he was eventually found and hanged.

- The short-term impact of the rebellion had white slave owners across the South terrified. This terror led many southern slave owners to use extremely harsh policies to deal with slaves and to prevent future insurrections.

Link it Back

In the early 1800s, former slave Denmark Vesey attempted to organize a revolt that might have included as many as 9,000 South Carolina slaves. His plan was foiled by a few slaves who feared being caught at the organizational meetings.

Link it Forward

In 1859, abolitionist John Brown conducted an unsuccessful raid on a federal arsenal at Harper's Ferry, VA. His intention was to arm slaves for a massive rebellion. He was caught and hanged.

NAT TURNER'S SLAVE REBELLION: 1831

Frederick Douglass

- At the age of twenty, Frederick Douglass escaped slavery and began a life as an influential abolitionist. His work included countless speeches that railed against slave policies, books that presented detailed narratives of slave life, and elegant essays that provided a narrative of the day-to-day injustices of enslaved and freed Blacks.

- Douglass's abolitionist newspaper, *The North Star,* was a major accomplishment. This widely distributed paper presented arguments against slavery, first-hand accounts from former slaves, and indictments against the federal government's inaction in terms of stopping the westward spread of slavery and ending the practice altogether.

- In the 1860s, Douglass served as an advisor to Abraham Lincoln on two separate occasions. Lincoln valued Douglass' views on abolition, as well as how the government could best assist newly freed slaves after the Civil War.

Link it Back

In 1830, William Lloyd Garrison published the abolitionist newspaper *The Liberator*. This publication told stories of the horrors of slavery, but became most famous for targeting the Constitution as a pro-slavery document as it was then written.

Link it Forward

In the 1890s, Douglass turned his attention to the fight against lynchings, which were taking place as white mobs were continuing to intimidate Blacks across the South.

Frederick Douglass

The Underground Railroad

- In the era leading up to the Civil War, the Underground Railroad represented the various routes that escaped slaves might take to gain their freedom in the North or in Canada. The Underground Railroad consisted of a coordinated group of abolitionist sympathizers who were usually already in the North or in states bordering the South. Some historians argue that the conductors, or those who helped the runaway slaves, take some of the credit away from the courageous slaves who did most of the work to escape.

- The most famous conductor was Harriet Tubman, herself an escaped slave. She made nineteen trips back to the South to help guide as many as three hundred slaves to freedom.

- The Underground Railroad shows that abolitionist groups were often well organized in their efforts to help fight slavery. Many of these abolitionists risked arrest and prison to take part in the struggle.

Link it Back

Some of the conductors of the railroad were Quakers. The Quakers, often from Pennsylvania, initiated a campaign against slavery shortly after the passage of the Constitution.

Link it Forward

The efforts of conductors infuriated southern slave owners. The Fugitive Slave Law was reinforced in 1850 to criminalize the act of aiding escaped slaves.

THE UNDERGROUND RAILROAD

Harriet Beecher Stowe — *Uncle Tom's Cabin*: 1852

- In 1852, Harriet Beecher Stowe wrote the novel, *Uncle Tom's Cabin*, as a response to the tightening of the Fugitive Slave Law, which mandated that northern police officers and government authorities work to return runaway slaves to their owners. Stowe encountered many runaway slaves while living in Cincinnati, Ohio.

- The book depicts the physical and emotional abuse that slaves encountered on southern plantations. It was widely read because many in the North and West did not know the details of slave life, and they were appalled by what they read. The book sold 300,000 copies in its first three months and was later turned into a popular play.

Link it Back

Stowe was the daughter of an abolitionist minister named Lyman Stowe. She credited her father's speeches and essays as the original influence for her book, as well as her own views on abolition.

Link it Forward

The book's influence on political thinking and the Civil War cannot be stressed enough. When Abraham Lincoln met Stowe in 1862, he said, "So this is the little lady who made this big war."

HARRIET BEECHER STOWE — UNCLE TOM'S CABIN : 1852

Sojourner Truth

- Sojourner Truth was an energetic abolitionist as well as a leader in the early women's rights movement. An escaped slave, Truth worked for the abolitionist movement, gathered supplies for the Union Army, and helped to recruit black soldiers for the North.

- She gave moving speeches for the anti-slavery movement, but is probably best known for her "Ain't I a Woman?" speech delivered to the Women's Convention in Ohio. There she spoke out for women's equality as well as the importance of women in the fabric of the American way of life. The speech also challenged Americans to show respect for hard working women and mothers. After the war, Truth spent her days campaigning against the racism endured by many freed men and women, including KKK attacks, lynchings, and poorly funded Freedmen's Bureaus.

Link it Back

Truth was a devout Christian. When Frederick Douglass suggested that God had abandoned Blacks, Truth responded with the famous quote, "Frederick, is God Dead?" Truth denounced the idea that God had left Blacks when they were in need.

Link it Forward

Though she never gained fame for it, Truth spent years speaking out against the government's lack of help for the nation's poor. Today, Sojourner Houses help women and families overcome poverty, addiction, and abuse.

Sojourner Truth

Compromise of 1850

- In 1850, the debate over the future of slavery was contentious. Southerners feared the addition of more free states because it could promote a federal ban on slavery and push the North and the South closer to conflict. With California's statehood looming, many wondered how the slave debate would play out in the western territories, where many sought statehood. If these territories became free states only, it could tip the balance of the Senate toward a free state majority.

- In the end, northerners and southerners worked out a compromise to satisfy both sides…for the time being. In the deal:

    ✓ <u>The North got</u>:

    - California admitted as a free state in 1850 and some territory in New Mexico back from Texas.

    - An end to the slave trade in Washington, DC.

    ✓ <u>The South got</u>:

    - A federal guarantee that citizens of the Utah and New Mexico territories could vote on slavery.

    - A tougher enforcement of the Fugitive Slave Law, which forced northern officials and police officers to return runaway slaves who had found their way to free states. The law had been in place for years, but it was rarely enforced.

    - Texas recuperated $10 million in compensation for the loss of New Mexico.

Link it Back

In the Missouri Compromise of 1820, it was decided that all land in the former Louisiana territory, above the 36', 30" line, would be free of slavery. California was not part of the Louisiana Territory.

Link it Forward

The South viewed the strengthening of the Fugitive Slave Law as a major victory in their quest for property rights over slaves. The North never fully enforced it, and Massachusetts actually tried to nullify it.

Compromise of 1850

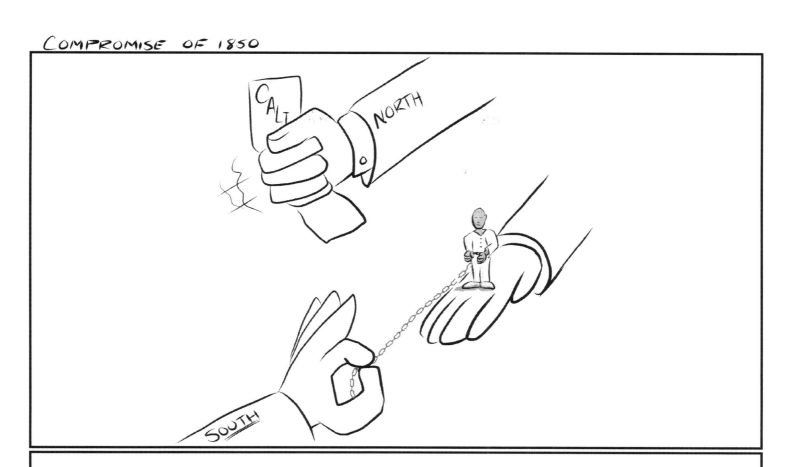

Kansas-Nebraska Act: 1854 / Bleeding Kansas: 1856

- Seeking to bring order to the Nebraska Territory so that a transcontinental rail line could be built through its land, Senator Stephen Douglas wanted to make Nebraska a state. Southerners objected because it would be a free state based on the Missouri Compromise and the 36', 30" line dividing free and slave states in the former Louisiana Territory.

- Since Douglas was seeking to gain southern support, he proposed repealing the Missouri Compromise, splitting the territory into two states (Kansas and Nebraska), and allowing the voters of the states to decide upon slavery (popular sovereignty). The law passed, but it was troubled from the start.

- Two unsettling things resulted from this law:

    ✓ Kansas was thrown into a virtual civil war when the vote to be a free or slave state was won by slave state proponents, even though they were dramatically outnumbered by free state proponents. Pro-slavery men had intimidated voters, and even shut down some polling places all together.

    ✓ Abolitionist John Brown and his men led the free-staters in a brutal campaign against pro-slavery Kansas men and Missouri's "border ruffians." This violent event is known as "Bleeding Kansas" and is considered by some as a preview of the Civil War.

    ✓ Many northerners were upset with Douglas and the Democrats for allowing slavery to move westward.

- The Kansas-Nebraska Act was one of the factors that led to the creation of the Republican Party. Republicans pledged to restrict the expansion of slavery. Many northern Democrats defected to the new party.

Link it Back

Territory gained in the war with Mexico had been free under Mexican law. In 1846, Pennsylvania Representative David Wilmot proposed legislation to ensure that slavery would be banned in lands claimed from the Mexican-American War. The "Wilmot Proviso" never became law, but it worked to create a clear division between northern and southern viewpoints.

Link it Forward

By the time Kansas gained statehood in 1861, the South had already seceded from the Union.

KANSAS - NEBRASKA ACT : 1854 / BLEEDING KANSAS : 1856

The Dred Scott Decision: 1857

- Dred Scott was a slave from Missouri (a slave state) who spent a number of years in both Illinois (free) and Minnesota (free) before he returned to Missouri. In 1846, Scott sued for his freedom because he had lived in free states for a prolonged period, and the Missouri Compromise had outlawed slavery in territories above the 36', 30" line. In 1857, the case finally made it to the Supreme Court. The court ruled that:

    ✓ The time in free territories DID NOT make Scott a free man.

    ✓ As a black man, free or slave, he was not eligible for citizenship, and could not appeal to the court for freedom.

    ✓ Congress never had the power to rule slavery illegal in any state because that would deny Americans their property rights given in the 5th Amendment. That made the Missouri Compromise, and the 36', 30" unconstitutional.

- Many northerners refused to accept this decision, and abolitionists across the US were irate over this victory for pro-slave southerners. Radical abolitionists, like John Brown, were now convinced that slavery could never be peacefully abolished. This was a significant step on the path to the Civil War.

Link it Back

One year earlier, Representative Preston Brooks (D-SC) beat Senator Charles Sumner (R-MA) with his cane for attacking Brooks' distant cousin, Andrew Butler (D-SC), in an anti-slave speech called "The Crime Against Kansas." Sumner received brain damage, while Brooks received new canes from fellow southerners showing their support for the assault. Things were heating up.

Link it Forward

In 1858, Abraham Lincoln made a push for the US Senate against rival Stephen Douglas. In one debate, Lincoln said, "A house divided against itself cannot stand. I believe this government cannot endure, permanently, half slave and half free." It was statements like these that led southerners to believe that President Lincoln would work to ban slavery.

The Dred Scott Decision: 1857

John Brown's Raid on Harper's Ferry: 1859

- In an attempt to steal weapons and arm slaves for a potential revolt on the Maryland-Virginia border, radical abolitionist John Brown raided a federal arsenal at Harper's Ferry, Virginia, in the fall of 1859. The raid was initially successful, but it was squashed days later by a company of Marines led by Colonel Robert E. Lee. Brown was captured, while his two sons were among ten of his followers who were killed in the battle with Lee's men.

- The raid foreshadowed the Civil War, which was now close at hand. Abolitionists applauded the actions of Brown, and southern officials and slave owners recognized that the potential for revolts and anti-slavery violence were increasing dramatically. John Brown was executed on December 2, 1859.

- Brown was viewed as a martyr for the cause of abolition by many Americans who were fighting against slavery.

Link it Back

Back in Kansas, Brown was involved in the Pottawatomie Massacre in which five pro-slavery settlers were murdered on the shores of Pottawatomie Creek.

Link it Forward

According to biographer Oswald Garrison Villard, John Brown's last words, written the day he hanged, were, "I, John Brown, am now quite certain that the crimes of this guilty land will never be purged away but with blood."

John Brown's Raid on Harper's Ferry: 1859

Election of 1860

- In the presidential election of 1860, the Democratic Party was a mess. Southern Democrats supported John Breckenridge while Democrats in the North and West supported Senator Stephen Douglas. Unfortunately for the Democrats, they both ran, and split the Democratic vote.

- The Republicans sensed an opportunity and ran Abraham Lincoln. Lincoln intended to expand federal power, spoke out against the expansion of slavery into western states, and would likely carry the swing state of Illinois, his home state, along with new western states.

- Lincoln won the election, even though he did not win a single southern state.

- Upon Lincoln's election in November, South Carolina seceded from the Union, fearing the increase in federal power and the potential outlawing of slavery (even though Lincoln had never specifically stated that intention). Mississippi, Florida, Alabama, Georgia, Louisiana, Texas, Virginia, Arkansas, North Carolina, and Tennessee broke away in the months to follow. This group formed the Confederate States of America under the guidance of President Jefferson Davis of Mississippi. Lines were now drawn.

Link it Back

In October 1858, in a debate at Knox College, Abraham Lincoln said, "Now I confess myself as belonging to that class in the country who contemplate slavery as a moral, social, and political evil."

Link it Forward

Some of the men who Lincoln had defeated in the race to be the Republican nominee for president became integral advisors in his cabinet. This group is known as his "Team of Rivals."

ELECTION OF 1860

Chapter 6

Chapter 6:

The Most Violent Event in American History Which We Continue to Re-Enact Every Weekend

The Attack on Fort Sumter: 1861

- Fort Sumter was built on a fortified island in the harbor off the coast of Charleston, South Carolina. The Union controlled this base when the South seceded in 1860-1861, but in the spring of 1861, it was in real danger from Confederate forces.

- Not wanting to get baited into being the aggressor in an armed conflict, Lincoln ordered the resupply of the fort but did not send in soldiers to reinforce the men at the base. In April of 1861, Confederate forces bombarded the fort and Union soldiers surrendered the following day. These were the first shots of the Civil War, and a small victory for the Confederacy, which would be defeated four years later.

Link it Back

During the Nullification Crisis of 1832, many observers thought that South Carolina was drawing the federal government into an armed crisis when they refused to pay a tariff on foreign goods. That crisis was averted.

Link it Forward

One of the Union commanders at the original siege of Fort Sumter was Abner Doubleday. Doubleday would be credited with inventing baseball, though that claim has been disputed.

THE ATTACK ON FORT SUMTER: 1861

Lincoln and the Income Tax: 1861

- In 1861, Lincoln imposed the first federal income tax by signing the Revenue Act. The revenue from this tax was used to equip Union troops, purchase weapons, and secure Washington, DC during the Civil War. Lincoln and Congress agreed to impose a 3% tax on annual incomes over $800.

- Many Republicans and Democrats questioned the legality of the tax, and it became another example of the federal government stretching its powers during a time of war in an effort to preserve national security.

Link it Back

Like income taxes, protective tariffs (taxes on imported goods) have been cloaked in controversy throughout American history. Tariffs are "protective" because the taxes on imported goods force foreign manufacturers to charge a higher rate, thus encouraging the consumption of American products. Those opposing tariffs believe that the tax reduces the competitiveness of the market, and allows American companies to charge higher prices which hurt consumers.

Link it Forward

The 16th Amendment, passed in 1913, made federal income tax a permanent fixture.

LINCOLN AND THE INCOME TAX: 1861

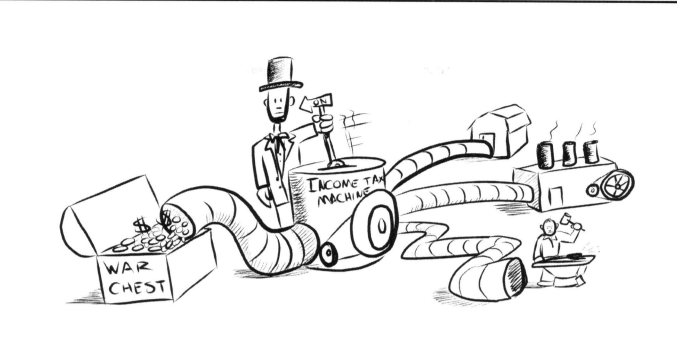

Lincoln and the Expansion of Executive Power: 1861 - 1865

- In 1861, Maryland State Legislator John Merryman was arrested for trying to halt a troop movement of Union soldiers. His attorney filed a writ of habeas corpus which would allow him to review evidence and charges against his client. Lincoln decided to suspend the writ of habeas corpus as a way of discouraging security breaches in border-states that might aid the rebellion in the South. Suspending habeas corpus would allow the government to imprison citizens without charging them with a crime. It was determined that Lincoln did not have this power.

- Later in the war, Lincoln's Secretary of War, Edwin Stanton, detained 350 men he believed to be dangerous to the war effort because they spoke out against Union leadership, the war, and the draft. These arrests were also ruled to be unconstitutional.

- Lincoln made an unsuccessful effort to support Stanton by pushing for military tribunals to try "war criminals," or those who attempted to impede Union efforts to reunite the nation. These tribunals allowed the courts to prevent the accused from having attorneys, bypass the jury system, and allow a three-judge panel to try and sentence Americans accused of treasonous actions. These tribunals would have denied the accused their 6th Amendment rights to an attorney and a trial by jury. Lincoln's attempt at military tribunals was halted by the courts.

Link it Back

President Andrew Jackson chose to disregard the Supreme Court ruling in the case of *Worchester v. Georgia* (1832). This ruling protected Cherokee land holdings, but Jackson forcibly removed the tribe anyway. This was known as the Trail of Tears.

Link it Forward

In 1933, Franklin D. Roosevelt proposed the largest expansion of federal and executive power in US history with his New Deal Programs. These programs involved massive government spending, and like Lincoln's plan to stretch executive power, Roosevelt's plan received frequent challenges from the courts.

LINCOLN AND THE EXPANSION OF EXECUTIVE POWER: 1861-1865

Battle of Antietam: 1862

- In 1862, Confederate General Robert E. Lee defied the Confederacy's defensive strategy and moved on Union troops under the direction of General George McClellan in Antietam, Maryland. Lee believed that this battle could give him control of this important area on the Maryland-Pennsylvania border.

- The fighting was brutal. Just over 22,000 soldiers were killed in the bloodiest one-day battle in American history. The battle was more or less a tie, but because Lee's troops retreated, the Union viewed it as a strategic victory. Shortly after this battle, President Lincoln removed General McClellan as general-in-chief for not pursuing Lee's scattered army and ending the war quickly with a decisive victory.

- The brutality of Antietam was the final justification Lincoln needed to submit the Emancipation Proclamation, which he felt would speed the end of the war by damaging the South's economy.

- With a number of generals failing to lead the Union to victory, General Ulysses S. Grant eventually became the general-in-chief of the Union Army, because Lincoln was impressed by his aggressive capture of Vicksburg, Mississippi. It was Grant who led Union troops to victory over the Confederacy.

Link it Back

Prior to Antietam, Lincoln supported McClellan, even though several members of his cabinet urged him to replace the Union commander with someone more aggressive.

Link it Forward

In 1951, President Harry S. Truman relieved General Douglas MacArthur of his command during the Korean War. MacArthur pushed for complete removal of communist forces in North Korea, whereas Truman sought to keep the war limited to avoid a full-scale conflict with China, and possibly the Soviet Union. The commander-in-chief won the argument.

Battle of Antietam : 1862

Emancipation Proclamation: 1863

- In 1863, Lincoln ordered the emancipation (freeing) of slaves in rebel states not controlled by the Union. He cited this as a "military necessity" and stated that he was acting as commander-in-chief of the US military.

- The unwritten goals of the proclamation were to:

    ✓ Encourage slave revolts and insurrection in the southern "rebel" states.

    ✓ Damage the southern economy by slowly diminishing their labor force.

    ✓ Encourage the recruitment of Blacks for the Union Army.

Link it Back

Lincoln stated in 1858, during his first debate with Stephen Douglass, that he had "no purpose, directly or indirectly, to interfere with the institution of slavery in the states where it exists." The Civil War, however, forced him to clearly address the slave issue, which divided the nation into the Union and the Confederacy.

Link it Forward

The Emancipation Proclamation did not officially free slaves, but it did change the focus of the war to being about something more than just the secession of the South. Slavery was officially outlawed by the 13th Amendment, passed in 1865.

Emancipation Proclamation: 1863

Civil War Draft Riots: 1863

- In 1863, Lincoln signed the National Conscription Act into law. The act made all single men (age twenty to forty-five), and married men (up to thirty-five), subject to a military draft lottery. One could avoid the draft by finding someone to replace them or paying a whopping fee of $300. Only the wealthiest citizens could afford that kind of payment.

- Lincoln had gained some public support for the war effort, but not in major cities like New York, where much of the immigrant population was called upon to fight a war that had little effect on their day-to-day lives. A draft riot, which broke out in New York City, was the deadliest in US history.

- Rioters targeted police and recruiting centers, and also sought out others they felt to be associated with the draft. They targeted Blacks because they saw them as the impetus for the war; they attacked the rich because of the $300 fee associated with avoiding the draft; and they targeted pro-Lincoln newspapers, such as *New York World*. They also attacked a number of businesses that profited from the war. Thousands died in the riot.

Link it Back

During the 1860 presidential campaign, in which Lincoln won, Democrats who opposed Lincoln warned northern city dwellers to prepare for a draft that would have them fighting a war in the South. Many ignored this threat, and Lincoln won every state in the Northeast in the election.

Link it Forward

In 1970, four college students were killed in a Vietnam War protest on the campus of Kent State University.

Civil War Draft Riots: 1863

"Gettysburg Address": 1863

- Over the course of three days, from July 1-3, 1863, the Battle of Gettysburg, fought in Pennsylvania, raged on until some 50,000 Americans lay dead. The Union was victorious and the Confederate Army retreated to Virginia. Lee's Army would never get that far north again.

- Local officials in Gettysburg created a national cemetery to honor the dead, and they asked Lincoln to open the grounds and honor the fallen troops. Lincoln chose this event to clarify his position on the rebellion and his policy toward the recreation of a united country.

- On November 19, 1863, roughly 15,000 people gathered to hear Lincoln speak. Many prepared to hear a typical Lincoln speech, which could last as long as two hours. The "Gettysburg Address" was 272 words long, and lasted less than three minutes. Lincoln opened the short speech by reminding Americans of the goals and values set forth by our Founding Fathers.

- He then spoke of imploring Americans to honor the dead by making sure that they work to unite the nation. He believed that the dead from BOTH sides would die in vain if the nation did not work to reunite in a peaceful manner. He believed that this devotion would ensure that a "government of the people, by the people, for the people, shall not perish from the earth."

Link it Back

In Lincoln's first inaugural address, he stated, "In your hands, my dissatisfied fellow-countrymen, and not in mine, is the momentous issue of civil war. The government will not assail you. You can have no conflict without being yourselves the aggressors. You have no oath registered in heaven to destroy the government, while I shall have the most solemn one to preserve, protect, and defend it."

Link it Forward

Lincoln's plan for forgiveness during post-Civil War reconstruction caused a great controversy with members of his own Republican Party. Many Republicans in Congress (often called Radical Republicans) wanted to punish the Confederacy for their rebellion. Lincoln believed that would lead to further division.

"GETTYSBURG ADDRESS": 1863

Sherman's March to the Sea: 1864

- In 1864, after destroying war resources in Rome, Georgia, General Sherman led his Union soldiers on a 265 mile march from Atlanta, Georgia to Savannah, Georgia. The purpose of this "March to the Sea" was to destroy southern morale by killing livestock, burning down farms, and salting the earth to destroy the soil.

- Sherman's effort was labeled as "total war," with the goal of demoralizing the civilians of the South and encouraging them to pressure Confederate officials into surrendering. Sherman's men adopted the motto "Make Georgia Howl" as a way of underscoring the need for brutality. After reaching Savannah, Sherman and his men turned north, marching through South Carolina and North Carolina.

Link it Back

Sherman was among a group of Civil War generals, including Lee, Grant, and Stonewall Jackson, who all attended the Military Academy at West Point. They were all very familiar with each other's battlefield tactics.

Link it Forward

Sherman later stated that he launched his total war because of his hatred for war. He believed that brutality would end the campaign faster. He later coined the phrase, "War is hell."

Sherman's March to the Sea: 1864

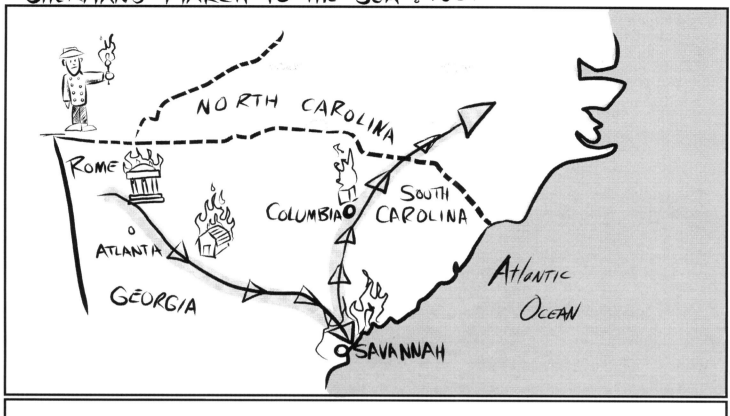

Chapter 7

Chapter 7:

A Couple Steps *FORWARD*, a Couple Steps BACK

Reconstruction Plans: Lincoln's Plan v. Radical Republicans' Plan

- Lincoln's proposal for Reconstruction included leniency toward the South in order to help restore order and peace in the US.

- Lincoln's plan called for:

    ✓ A general amnesty (forgiveness) to be granted to all southerners who would take an oath of loyalty to the United States and pledge to obey all federal laws pertaining to slavery.

    ✓ Temporarily excluding Confederate officials and military leaders from the readmission process.

    ✓ Allowing southern state re-admission, recreation of government, and elected officials in Congress once 10% of the number of voters who had participated in the 1860 election had taken the oath of loyalty within a particular state.

- The plan of Radical Republicans, such as Thaddeus Stevens, was to punish the South for their rebellion. Radical Republicans believed that the South should be treated as a conquered territory.

- This Radical Republican plan called for:

    ✓ Military governors to rule southern states.

    ✓ A majority of citizens (51%) to be required to take a loyalty oath before the readmission process could begin.

Link it Back

Lincoln's Plan clearly reflected his ideas presented in the "Gettysburg Address" by detailing the need for a nation united as one.

Link it Forward

The glaring differences in reconstruction plans foreshadowed the impeachment of President Andrew Johnson, who worked to implement Lincoln's plan, though he never reached Lincoln's level of credibility.

Reconstruction Plans: Lincoln's Plan v. Radical Republicans' Plan

The Assassination of Abraham Lincoln: 1865

- On April 14th, 1865, Abraham Lincoln and his wife, Mary Todd Lincoln, attended a play at Ford's Theater in Washington, DC. A Virginia man named John Wilkes Booth entered Lincoln's private box and shot him.

- On the morning of April 15th, Lincoln died as law enforcement pursued Booth and his co-conspirators. Vice President Andrew Johnson was sworn in as president, and on April 26th, Booth and his accomplices were captured. They were all hanged on July 7th.

Link it Back

Lincoln pressured Congress to progress the 13th Amendment (abolishment of slavery) toward ratification. His influence helped to move the amendment through Congress, but he did not live to see it officially enacted.

Link it Forward

The US Secret Service was created by Lincoln in 1865, but it was not formally introduced until July of 1865 (three months after Lincoln's death). The Secret Service was set up to pursue counterfeiters, and was not called into protection duty until after President William McKinley was assassinated in 1901.

The Assassination of Abraham Lincoln: 1865

Impeachment of President Andrew Johnson: 1868

- President Johnson carried on a version of Lincoln's plan for reconstruction, which included:

    ✓ Nearly total amnesty to ex-Confederates.

    ✓ Rapid restoration of state status for seceded states.

    ✓ Re-establishment of local southern governments.

- Unfortunately for Johnson and southern Blacks, local governments were able to enact Black Codes, which limited the rights of newly freed slaves through systematic segregation.

- Republicans in Congress earned the nickname "Radical Republicans" because of their desire to punish the southerners for their rebellion and other acts of treason. They pushed Lincoln, right up to the time of his death, to punish the South.

- The Radicals did not care for Johnson's lenient attitude toward the South's re-admission to the Union. When Johnson sought to remove Secretary of War Edwin Stanton, even though he was approved by the Senate, the Radical Republicans in the House called this a violation of the Tenure of Office Act, and they impeached him. In his impeachment trial in the Senate, Johnson avoided being removed from office by one vote.

- For the remainder of his term Johnson had almost no credibility with members of Congress, and it was his own party (Republicans) who led the charge to have him removed from office. The Radical Republicans had almost nothing stopping them from implementing restrictive laws on southern readmission to the Union.

Link it Back

Radicals Republicans, led by Thaddeus Stevens, wanted a weakened South, which they could control, and they wanted Republican control of Congress for the era of Civil War Reconstruction. The Radicals saw Johnson as weak, and they sought to limit his power from the start of his presidency.

Link it Forward

Following Johnson's impeachment, Congress increased the US military presence in the South, and controlled the gradual re-admission of southern states back into the Union.

IMPEACHMENT OF PRESIDENT ANDREW JOHNSON: 1868

The Formation of the KKK: 1866

- Following the Civil War, some white southerners feared a rise in the political power of former slaves, which would impede the supremacy of white landholders. The Ku Klux Klan (KKK) was formed as a terrorist group that focused its intimidation at newly freed Blacks as well as Republican leaders who aimed to empower former slaves and black voters (after the 15th Amendment was established in 1870). The KKK burned crosses at black churches and homes, and they orchestrated hundreds of lynchings across the South.

- Though the era of Jim Crow segregation laws did not officially begin until the Reconstruction period ended, the federal government's lack of action against KKK initiatives seemed to condone many of the South's racially oppressive policies, like the Black Codes. Black Codes laid out very strict guidelines for the separation of newly freed slaves from Whites. These guidelines included separate schools, no interracial marriages, and the need for freed men to prove that they were working in order to stay in a particular area.

- Many historians believe that the lack of federal intervention against the Klan, as well as the passage of Black Codes, led to the creation of Jim Crow policies across the South.

Link it Back

The passage of the 13th Amendment, which ended slavery, was a major motivating factor for some Whites in the South to form the KKK. Many Klan members believed that federal voting laws were not far behind, and they were right. The 15th Amendment (black males voting) was passed in 1870.

Link it Forward

At the end of the Reconstruction Era, the power and influence of the KKK dropped off significantly. The KKK rose again in the 1920s as a nativist group that aimed to stop the influence of groups such as immigrants, Jews, and Catholics.

THE FORMATION OF THE KKK: 1866

The Civil War Amendments — 13th, 14th, and 15th

- The 13th, 14th, and 15th Amendments were post-war additions to the Constitution meant to provide Blacks (black men, in particular) with the full rights and citizenship of white male Americans.

- <u>13th Amendment</u>:

    ✓ Freed slaves throughout the entire US and made slavery permanently illegal.

- <u>14th Amendment</u>:

    ✓ Gave citizenship to all Americans regardless of race.

    ✓ Protected Americans against unfair state actions.

    ✓ Guaranteed that no person could be deprived of due process of law.

    ✓ Guaranteed equal protection under the law to ALL Americans.

- <u>15th Amendment</u>:

    ✓ Gave black males the right to vote.

Link it Back

The Emancipation Proclamation freed slaves in rebel (Confederate) states. This order was meant to cripple the South's economy and cause slave revolts across the Confederacy.

Link it Forward

The Civil Rights Act of 1964 was passed to ensure the federal government protected Blacks against the Jim Crow Laws, which denied Blacks many rights and freedoms, including the right to vote.

THE CIVIL WAR AMENDMENTS — 13th, 14th, AND 15th

Freedmen's Bureaus: 1865 - 1872

- Freedmen's Bureaus were created in 1865 by President Lincoln. They were set up to ease the transition from slavery to free life for Blacks in the South. Early on, they provided basic needs, education for children, and some job training. The bureaus were also supposed to help redistribute confiscated southern land to freedmen.

- Unfortunately, Freedmen's Bureaus were ineffective. They were poorly funded, undermanned, and easily intimidated by the KKK and other radical groups. After Lincoln's assassination, President Johnson's soft policies on the South made it difficult for the federal government to assist the bureaus. This meant that a lot of former slaves returned to plantations as "sharecroppers," which was simply a version of financial slavery.

- Though this initiative provided funds for the construction of schools, and in some cases, paid the salaries of teachers who helped to create black schools, the Freedmen's Bureaus were a failure because of the lack of follow-through by Presidents Johnson and Grant.

Link it Back

In creating the Emancipation Proclamation of 1863, Lincoln recognized that the transition to free life for Blacks would be difficult. When the Proclamation was enacted, he began conceiving a plan to provide freed slaves with the social and economic basics to start a new life.

Link it Forward

The ineffectiveness of federal agencies prompted men like Booker T. Washington to take the lead in creating "self-help" for Blacks in the form of schools, such as the Tuskegee Institute.

Freedmen's Bureaus: 1865-1872

Jim Crow Voting Laws

- In 1877, Reconstruction and its harsh policies directed at the South came to a close. State governments across the South, fearing the voting power of newly freed black males, created Jim Crow policies to keep Blacks and Whites separated, and to limit the voting power of Blacks. Some examples of Jim Crow voting laws were:

    ✓ <u>Literacy Tests:</u> Voters in the South were made to read passages from books to prove they were literate, and thusly prove that they could vote. Blacks and poor Whites often had to read passages from medical books, while land owning Whites read from children's books, or not at all.

    ✓ <u>Poll Taxes:</u> Poll taxes were a tax that state and local governments required from citizens in exchange for the ability to vote. Once again, poor Whites and Blacks were disenfranchised by the tax.

    ✓ <u>Grandfather Clause:</u> If an American enjoyed full voting status prior to 1866, they were exempt from some of the poll taxes and literacy tests that limited voting rights. Blacks were not given full voting rights until the 15th Amendment was passed in 1870.

Link it Back

In 1866, as soon as the Civil War ended, many states instituted Black Codes, which laid out very strict guidelines for the separation of newly freed slaves and Whites. These guidelines included separate schools, no interracial marriages, and the need for freedmen to prove that they were working in order to stay in a particular area.

Link it Forward

It took until 1964 for the federal government to outlaw poll taxes with the 24th Amendment.

Jim Crow Voting Laws

Plessy v. Ferguson: 1896

- In 1892, Homer A. Plessy boarded a train in Louisiana. He purchased a first class ticket to sit in the all-white train car, even though he was 1/8 black (which, by law, made him black). He was asked to give up his seat, and was arrested when he refused to do so. He was imprisoned by a local judge named John H. Ferguson.

- Plessy appealed the case, arguing that the Separate Car Act of Louisiana, which separated Blacks and Whites on trains, was unconstitutional based on the 14th Amendment's Equal Protection Clause. This clause guarantees all citizens of the US equal protection under the law.

- The Supreme Court's famous 1896 ruling on the case was "Separate, but Equal." The court determined that if all factors are equal, then segregation is justified because it is used for the "preservation of public peace and good order." The court was making the determination that the country was simply not ready for full desegregation in the late 1800s.

Link it Back

One could argue that the 14th Amendment was set up to combat the practices of segregation in the South. The 14th provides for:
- Citizenship for African-Americans.
- Equal protection for all citizens.
- Protection from unfair state actions.
- A guarantee of due process of law.

Link it Forward

A 1954 case, *Brown v. Board of Education of Topeka,* overturned the *Plessy* case. In this case, segregation laws that separated school children in Kansas were ruled unconstitutional because the separation was not equal in terms of facilities, licensed teachers, and classroom materials.

Plessy v. Ferguson : 1896

Booker T. Washington and W.E.B. Dubois

Booker T. Washington

- Washington was a controversial Black leader who rose out of the Reconstruction era to help guide Blacks toward economic and political freedom. Washington believed that if Blacks could become economically independent from Whites, they would be accepted by the white-dominated American culture.

- Washington became president of the Tuskegee Institute and made it a prominent vocational college where young black men learned valuable job skills to pursue Washington's dream of creating a society of economically independent Blacks.

- Washington took heavy criticism for his *Atlanta Compromise* in which he argued that Blacks should accept disenfranchisement and social segregation as long as Whites allow them economic progress, educational opportunity, and justice in the courts. Critics argued that lowered expectations would not help Blacks achieve equality and civil rights. Washington went on to become an advisor for both Presidents Theodore Roosevelt and William Taft.

W.E.B. Dubois

- Dubois was the first black man to receive a doctoral degree from Harvard University. He argued strongly against Washington's *Atlanta Compromise* because it did not push for full equality for Blacks.

- Dubois also argued that Blacks needed to focus on education as a way to become part of the solutions that move Blacks in America toward equal standing with Whites. Dubois wrote about this in his book of essays, *The Souls of Black Folks*, which argued against the biological and intellectual superiority of Whites.

- Dubois founded the National Association for the Advancement of Colored People (NAACP), an organization that focused on civil rights issues such as voting rights, Jim Crow laws, and anti-lynching laws.

Link it Back

Most of the issues black men dealt with should have been taken care of by the 13th, 14th, and 15th Amendments, but the federal government failed to properly enforce these constitutional changes.

Link it Forward

A group of Tuskegee Institute students and graduates became known as the Tuskegee Airmen during WWII. These were America's first black combat pilots and airmen, and they earned numerous medals for bravery and service.

BOOKER T. WASHINGTON AND W.E.B. DUBOIS

Chapter 8

Chapter 8:

America Moves Leftward

Manifest Destiny: Mid - Late 1800s

- Columnist John L. O'Sullivan claimed that westward expansion was, "our manifest destiny to over spread the continent allotted by Providence for the free development of our yearly multiplying millions." In other words, Americans needed to expand to the Pacific Ocean, seize lands even if they were owned by Native American tribes, and develop an advanced agricultural and industrial society in the West.

- The reasons for westward expansion included:

    ✓ A general overcrowding in eastern cities such as New York and Philadelphia.

    ✓ The lure of the Homestead Act of 1862, which granted 160 acres of government land to citizens willing to settle in the West.

    ✓ A lack of respect for Native American tribes and their lands. The US government saw protecting settlers as an excuse to establish dominance over native tribes.

    ✓ The expansion of the US economy and the need to explore new resources that might be available in the western portion of the country.

- The people who moved westward included land speculators, farmers, ranchers, minors, rail workers, and homesteaders.

Link it Back

The Northwest Ordinance of 1787 included procedures for creating new states that were not part of the original thirteen colonies. That procedure was used to establish states in the western frontier.

Link it Forward

The same sense of destiny and expansionism were the motivations for American imperialism in the late 1800s and early 1900s. The US expanded its influence in Latin America and Asia during this era.

MANIFEST DESTINY: MID-LATE 1800s

Transcontinental Railroad: 1862 - 1869

- In 1862, President Abraham Lincoln signed the Pacific Railway Act, which provided federal funding for a rail line linking the east and west coasts. The act chartered the Central Pacific and the Union Pacific Railroad Companies to complete the line. The Central Pacific Railroad Company would start building in Sacramento, California (heading east), while the Union Pacific Railroad Company would begin on the Missouri River (heading west).

- The rail line was a financial boom for the companies. Each received $48,000 in government bonds for every mile completed, causing some of the construction supervisors to choose curved rather than straight lines for the rails. The railroad line took seven years to build and made tens of millions of dollars for men such as Leland Stanford and Dr. Thomas Durant.

- Temporary settlements popped up wherever the line moved, and often gambling, prostitution, and heavy drinking took place. The line was also repeatedly attacked by various Native American tribes who were concerned about White infringement upon tribal lands.

- Whites used advanced weapons to control large groups of Natives Americans, while the alcohol they brought had life-threatening consequences for natives, who had little to no tolerance of its physical effects. The new settlers used barbed wire to divide land and control livestock, but the wiring, as well as the rifles, killed thousands of buffalo, which were an important food source for Native Americans.

- Thousands of Chinese immigrants were hired to complete tough manual labor, detonate TNT (explosives), and pound rail spikes. The two rail companies' lines finally met in 1869, at Promontory Summit in Utah. One could now travel by rail from major east coast cities all the way to California.

Link it Back

There was a push in the 1840s to begin a transcontinental railroad with the onset of the Manifest Destiny movement, but the heated sectionalism of the era took the government's focus away from westward expansion.

Link it Forward

The Credit Mobilier Company was formed by Union Pacific (UP) stockholders. UP then gave contracts to the Credit Mobilier Corporation to do rail work. Congressmen were given shares in Credit Mobilier in order to guarantee that federal funding was provided for the Transcontinental Railroad. The Credit Mobilier Scandal cost many politicians their jobs, and some even received jail time.

TRANSCONTINENTAL RAILROAD: 1862-1869

Homestead Act: 1862

- In 1862, Congress passed the Homestead Act to encourage westward expansion beyond the Mississippi River. The law stated that citizens, or those working toward citizenship, could apply to receive a land grant of 160 acres that would be free of cost if they stayed on the property for at least five years.

- The act was effective in helping to settle the West and to provide opportunities for impoverished farmers from the East to start anew. Nearly 1.6 million claims were approved while the act was in existence. Unfortunately, much of the land was gobbled up by land speculators and railroad companies who hoarded the land, and, eventually, drove up prices on the property.

- As settlers flooded the Great Plains, Native Americans, who had been continuously pushed westward, fought back. This resistance led to the decades-long Indian Wars, and finally, tribal submissions to federal authority.

Link it Back

The over 9,600,000 acres claimed by "Homesteaders" were part of the former Louisiana Territory, purchased by Thomas Jefferson sixty years earlier.

Link it Forward

The land speculation and the expansion of rail companies resulting from the Homestead Act led farmers and ranchers to create a political organization called the Grange. The Grange worked to give farmers and ranchers a political voice, limit the illegal sale of Homestead lands, and regulate the monopolistic practices of railroads and warehouse companies.

Homestead Act: 1862

The Dawes Act: 1887

- The Dawes Act was passed in order to integrate Native Americans into white culture and break up massive Native American reservations. The new reservations were to be divided into smaller 160-acre land holdings to encourage farming and smaller family units, which were customary in white culture. It also provided an opportunity for Whites moving westward, as well as railroad companies, to purchase huge chunks of tribal land which were now available for sale.

- This law was a disaster for Native Americans. Boarding schools punished students for speaking tribal languages or behaving in manners which were considered non-white. Native land holding in the West dropped from 138 million acres in 1887 to 78 million acres in 1990, as land was being purchased by white settlers and speculators. In many ways, the act slowly destroyed ancient tribal customs and the native tradition of living with extended families for support.

Link it Back

During the Revolutionary War, Native American tribes fought alongside the British. Even though the tribes were mainly fighting for land claims, as well as self-determination, their reputation as being anti-American may have been too much to overcome.

Link it Forward

The Dawes Act was repealed in 1934, but the federal government ruled that land purchased as a result of the act would not have to be returned to Native American tribes.

The Dawes Act: 1887

The Grange

- The Grange was an organization started by mid-western and western farmers and ranchers originally intending to communicate new agricultural practices. It developed into a political organization and lobbyist group that voiced displeasure with inflated warehouse and rail rates they believed were crippling traditional family farms.

- The Grange eventually created "Granger Laws" which specifically called for the government to regulate the monopolistic business practices of railroad companies, meat packers, and storage companies. The pinnacle of these laws was the Interstate Commerce Act of 1887, which set up the federal government's regulation of railroad price-fixing.

Link it Back

Thomas Jefferson feared that an industrialized America could interfere with the simple freedoms of an agricultural society. Jefferson supported farmers because he knew that with industry came the greed of laissez-faire (little to no government regulation) capitalism, which often oppressed those in the lower and middle classes.

Link it Forward

The late 1800s began an age of monopolies and the industrial giants who operated them. Men like Rockefeller (oil), Carnegie (steel), and Morgan (railroads) used government deregulation as a way to control huge markets, abuse workers, and raise prices. Controlling these businesses and their practices was a difficult task for the federal government.

THE GRANGE

Munn v. Illinois: 1877

- In 1871, the warehouse firm of Munn and Scott was found guilty of violating state laws which regulated warehouses prices. The firm appealed the ruling by arguing that the Illinois state government's regulation of industry was unconstitutional because it resulted in the deprivation of property without due process of law as required by the 5th and 14th Amendments. In other words, warehouse owners believed that government regulations did not allow them to make the amount of profit that they could have without the regulations.

- The appeal made it to the Supreme Court in 1877, and the court sided with Illinois because regulating businesses tied to farming had a direct impact on the public interest (food sources). This was a MAJOR victory for those in support of government regulation of businesses.

Link it Back

As in the case of *Gibbons v. Ogden* (1824), the court cited the Commerce Clause of the Constitution which states that Congress has the power "to regulate commerce with foreign nations and among the several States." The court ruled that the State House of Illinois enjoyed that same power.

Link it Forward

In 1911, the Supreme Court heard the case of *Standard Oil Company of New Jersey v. United States*. The court ruled that Standard Oil had intentionally entered into contracts that allowed them to monopolize oil production in the US. Standard Oil was one of the most powerful monopolies of its time.

MUNN V. ILLINOIS: 1877

American Populism

- The Populist Movement was spurred by mid-western farmers and ranchers who wanted to have their simple family farm life protected from the power and influence of major corporations and powerful government officials. The movement eventually included eastern laborers, and some elements of populism led to the Progressive Movement of the late 1800s and early 1900s.

- Populists strived for:

    ✓ A graduated income tax, which placed a larger portion of the US tax burden onto the wealthy.

    ✓ A move away from the gold standard (money backed by gold), which they believe over-valued money and made it difficult to pay off bank loans. Populists pushed for "bi-metalism" which had money backed by silver and gold in order to stabilize currency and promote its circulation.

    ✓ An amendment to the Constitution that allowed for the direct election of senators so that common people could have a voice in selecting all of their federal representatives to Congress.

    ✓ State initiatives to allow citizens to propose laws, which gave the people a larger voice in state and local policy-making.

Link it Back

In 1903, L. Frank Baum published *The Wizard of Oz* to the delight of millions. Baum was a vocal populist of the late 1800s, and many people believe that the book is an allegory of the Populist Movement with nearly all characters representing people and issues of the era.

Link it Forward

The 17th Amendment (1913) legislated the direct election of senators and was seen by many populists and progressives as a major political victory for common Americans. Before that, state legislators chose one of their own members to be a US senator, instead of having the people of the state vote directly to send a candidate to Washington, DC. The process was perceived as corrupt and elitist.

AMERICAN POPULISM

Chapter 9

Chapter 9:

Mo' Money...
Mo' Labor Disputes

Robber Barons or Captains of Industry

- John D. Rockefeller – (Standard Oil Company) Rockefeller was once known as the wealthiest American. He created a multi-million dollar oil industry through the process of horizontal consolidation, which is buying out one's competitors in order to control a particular market. Rockefeller was known for his brutal business tactics and oppressive treatment of labor, but also for large philanthropic gifts (donations) to various charities and foundations.

- Cornelius Vanderbilt – (Shipping, then Railroads) Vanderbilt built a shipping empire that dominated east coast waterways. Toward the end of his career, he began investing heavily in railroad lines and eventually turned the business over to his son William. Like Rockefeller, Vanderbilt was a philanthropist. Vanderbilt University is named for him.

- Andrew Carnegie – (Steel) Carnegie was a Scottish immigrant who built the most powerful steel industry in the world. He used vertical integration, which is the process of buying out his suppliers and distributors in order to control the costs of production and shipping. Carnegie employed thousands (though he oppressed most of the workers), made millions, and donated huge sums of money.

- J.P. Morgan – (Corporate finance in railroads and steel) Morgan financed many east coast railroads, which he turned into monopolies by pushing out the competition with low rates. He then raised the rates after eliminating the competition in order to make up for lost profits. He used his fortune to create US Steel, which was purchased from Carnegie. The US government even asked for Morgan's help to bail them out of a late 19th century economic crisis.

These men were sometimes referred to as robber barons because they abused workers and manipulated prices through monopolies and trusts. Others saw these men as captains of industry because they provided jobs, built useful industries, and donated millions to various foundations and charities.

Link it Back

The laissez-faire policies of the post-reconstruction era helped the US build a massive industrial machine, but it also led to some of the practices that created trusts and monopolies. These practices eliminated all but a tiny amount of competition and promoted high prices and poor working conditions.

Link it Forward

The Sherman Anti-Trust Act of 1890 and the Clayton Anti-Trust Act of 1914 are two laws that illustrate how the federal government worked to regulate monopolies and trusts that ended up hurting laborers and consumers.

Robber Barons or Captains of Industry

American Innovators at the Turn of the Century

- <u>Thomas Edison, The Wizard of Menlo Park (NJ)</u>: Edison is credited with 1,001 federal patents. Some of his most significant inventions include the incandescent light bulb, the phonograph (record player), the movie camera, and electricity distribution.

- <u>George Eastman</u>: While French inventor Nicephore Niepce produced the first photographic image in the world, it was Eastman who created cameras (the Kodak and the Brownie) that were affordable and easily used by the common person. By the late 1920s, Eastman Kodak Co. was the largest camera manufacturer in the world.

- <u>Alexander Graham Bell</u>: A Scottish-born American inventor who, while trying to create telegraphic speech by using electrical currents, "accidentally" invented the telephone in 1875. "Accidentally," because he did not intend to transmit sounds the way he did.

- <u>The Wright Brothers</u>: Inventors from Dayton, OH, the Wrights traveled to Kittyhawk, NC, in 1903 in order to test their "flying machine." While the first machine-powered flight lasted only 12 seconds, three tries later they were able to get a plane to stay in the air for 59 seconds. The Wright Brothers not only patented the airplane, they patented flight.

Link it Back

Patent protection is spelled out in Article II of the Constitution. Patents offer certain rights to an inventor for up to twenty years, during which time the inventor may exclude all others from making, using, importing, or selling his or her invention.

Link it Forward

Edison helped found Con-Edison, which provides power to downstate NY. Eastman founded the Eastman Kodak Co., which made affordable cameras and camera film. Bell helped to create what is now known as AT&T. The Wright Brothers had a difficult time establishing the legitimacy of their invention, and never really founded a significant airline.

American Innovators at the Turn of the Century

Haymarket Affair: 1886

- For several days, workers at the McCormick Reaper Works in Chicago, IL went on strike to protest wage cuts as well as job losses due to an increased use of machinery on the manufacturing line. These workers were members of the labor union known as the Knights of Labor. During the protests, a number of strikers were injured by Chicago Police who feared the strike could become a riot, and a number of officers were also injured.

- Later that week, signs were posted asking workers to meet at Haymarket Square to protest the violence of the Chicago Police Department. Police also arrived when rumors spread that anarchists were among the strikers and their goal was to take down the city's government, not just the McCormick plant.

- Shortly after the meeting began, police closed in. An anarchist threw a bomb into the crowd, killing eight people. Seven of the dead were police officers. Public opinion of unions fell to an all-time low, and this incident made many government officials realize that it would take more than the local police to stop these strikes.

Link it Back

Much of the controversy in Chicago was about wages, but some of it was connected to the implementation of an eight-hour work day. In 1867, the Illinois House passed a mandated eight-hour work day maximum, but employers simply refused to obey the law, which was poorly enforced.

Link it Forward

In 1935, President Roosevelt signed the National Labor Relations Act, also called the Wagner Act. This law made collective bargaining between labor and management legal. Workers could no longer be fired or penalized for being members of a union.

HAYMARKET AFFAIR: 1886

Rise of Major Unions at the Turn of the Century

- In 1886, Samuel Gompers established the American Federation of Labor (AFL). The AFL was formed to organize skilled workers, such as carpenters and masons, across the US. This union helped to set up collective bargaining between labor and ownership, and to strive for appropriate wages and working conditions for their craftspeople.

- In 1905, the Industrial Workers of the World (IWW) was formed by renown socialist Eugene Debs as a labor organization for various unskilled workers. Nicknamed "Wobblies," these workers included miners, loggers, factory labor, and even some farm hands. The IWW fought for better wages and working conditions.

- Unions of unskilled laborers, like the IWW, were often prone to advocating strikes and picketing (organized demonstrations against a business) because their workers could be replaced with relative ease by many employers. These activities could make them highly unpopular with both business leaders and the American public, who often saw their actions as anti-American and anti-capitalist. Unions were sometimes associated with socialism and radical acts.

Link it Back

The IWW sought to keep itself from being linked to another unskilled labor union, the Knights of Labor. The Knights of Labor became virtually extinct after the Haymarket Affair in Chicago, which killed a number of police officers.

Link it Forward

In 1955, the AFL merged with the Congress of Industrial Organizations (CIO) to form the largest union in American history (AFL-CIO). The CIO consisted primarily of skilled and unskilled industrial laborers.

Rise of Major Unions at the Turn of the Century

Union Turmoil at the Turn of the Century

Strike: A refusal to continue working because workers, or their labor union, cannot come to an agreement regarding wages or proper working conditions.

- The Great Strike of 1877: In 1877, workers for the Baltimore & Ohio Railroad went on strike because of significant pay cuts. These strikes became violent, and though state militias were brought in to quell the violence, they were ineffective. President Hayes was forced to send in federal troops to restore order in places like West Virginia and Pittsburgh, PA. This was the first time federal soldiers were used to end a labor strike.

- Homestead Lockout: In 1892, a dispute between Carnegie Steel and the Amalgamated Association of Iron and Steel Workers erupted over a contract that favored the union and its workers. Plant manager William Clay Frick locked out employees (refused to allow them to work under the new contract) and violence erupted between private Pinkerton police officers, who were hired by Carnegie, and the union. Sixteen people were killed before the Pennsylvania State Militia stopped the violence.

- Pullman Strike: In 1894, laborers went on strike against the Pullman Car Company because they refused to take a pay cut. Pullman fired 5,000 employees. In response, rail company labor unions asked companies not to use Pullman cars on their lines. When the court ruled that tactic to be illegal, violence erupted, and the army was called in to stop the strikers.

Link it Back

Unions struggled against the corporations that paid low wages and had poor working conditions, but also the government's support of those corporations.

Link it Forward

In 1902, President Theodore Roosevelt helped to mediate an agreement between labor and ownership in the Anthracite Coal Strike. Momentum and public support had shifted toward the unions, and Roosevelt chose not to use military force to put down strikes.

Union Turmoil At The Turn Of The Century

Political Machines of the Late 19th Century

- Major cities like New York and Chicago had poorly organized local governments that struggled to provide basic services for the massive poor and immigrant populations of the mid-to-late 1800s. Political machines, such as the Tammany Hall organization, which was run by underhanded Democrats in New York City, were political groups that dominated city governments with a systematic form of corruption.

- The Tammany Hall machine worked like this:

    ✓ Tammany operator Boss Tweed, and other machine workers, would make contact with immigrants, sometimes right at the docks. They would offer them food, medical help, and jobs in exchange for votes for Tammany (Democrats).

    ✓ The factories working with Tammany would employ these immigrants, and they would be rewarded with BIG money government contracts pushed through by Tweed.

    ✓ The businesses would then provide Boss Tweed with a "kickback" (illegal cash bribe) for the awarding of the lucrative contracts, and also to make sure they stayed in his good graces.

    ✓ Immigrants voted for Tammany at the polls as a way of showing their appreciation for the assistance, and the system got stronger. This is organized corruption.

Link it Back

Immigrants were drawn to major cities like New York because of the availability of factory jobs. New York was one of several northeastern cities at the center of the American Industrial Revolution.

Link it Forward

Political machines were yet another example of the corruption leading up to the Progressive Movement, which sought to limit the power of big businesses and criminals in government, while returning power to common laborers and law-abiding citizens.

Political Machines of the Late 19th Century

Triangle Shirtwaist Fire: 1911

- A fire broke out at a New York City sweatshop that employed mostly young immigrant women as seamstresses. These women endured low wages, horrible working conditions, and almost non-existent safety standards.

- As the fire spread between the 9th and the 11th floors, many of the women realized that escape exits were chained or blocked. When smoke filled the unventilated rooms, dozens of women went out onto the fire escape to seek safety. The fire escape collapsed killing dozens of workers. In the end, 129 women and 17 men died from burns, smoke inhalation, or the impact of falling or jumping.

- This incident drew many Americans' attention to the issues of workers' rights, lack of womens' voices in politics (suffrage), and the need for government safety standards in industry: all factors that contributed to this horrific tragedy.

Link it Back

Many immigrants came to live in major cities because of the availability of factory jobs. The limited availability of jobs for women allowed some employers to force them to endure horrible working conditions.

Link it Forward

Dozens of fire codes and safety laws were established in New York City following the Triangle Shirtwaist Fire. It took almost another full decade for women to be granted the right to vote for the men who created and enforced these codes and laws.

TRIANGLE SHIRTWAIST FIRE: 1911

Chapter 10

Chapter 10:

Send Us Your Huddled Masses to STOP SENDING US YOUR HUDDLED MASSES

US Immigration: 1870 - 1920

- Historians estimate that between 20 and 40 million immigrants arrived in America between 1870 and 1920. These immigrants usually came from Europe and Asia, and they were generally part of the working poor.

- The mass immigation of the era reflected America's need for laborers during the rapid industrialization of the US after the Reconstruction. These immigrants often settled in cities, and many of them gained employment in factories and mines on the East Coast.

- Not all Americans were happy about immigration. Nativists and union leaders worried about resident Americans losing their jobs to immigrants willing to work for less pay.

Link it Back

The Irish Potato Famine of the late 1840s pushed many Irish citizens to seek a new home in the states during the 1850s and 1860s.

Link it Forward

Immigration policy has always been controversial. Government officials in the 21st century have had a difficult time agreeing on how to stop illegal immigration, take care of the children of illegal immigrants, and provide some immigrants with a legal pathway to citizenship.

US IMMIGRATION: 1870-1920

New Immigrants v. Old Immigrants: 1870 - 1920

- The "old" immigrants came to the US prior to 1870 and tended to be:

    ✓ Protestant and from Northern/Western Europe.

- The "new" immigrants who came after 1870 were often:

    ✓ Jewish, Catholic, or Buddhist and from Eastern Europe or Asia.

- New immigrants were looked down upon by many old immigrants. Some new immigrant groups set up their own neighborhoods in cities for protection and security. Chinatown and Little Italy are examples of these communities.

Link it Back

Native Americans were not included in the debate between "old" and "new" immigrants, even though they had been removed from their ancestral lands and relocated to reservations across much of the Midwest.

Link it Forward

The "new" immigrants under the most scrutiny were often Asians. Starting in 1882, the US government passed a series of Chinese Exclusion Acts that restricted, and then entirely banned, Chinese immigration for decades.

NEW IMMIGRANTS V. OLD IMMIGRANTS: 1870-1920

Nativism — The Anti-Immigration Movement

- The Nativist Movement began in the 1840s as a way for groups, primarily in large eastern cities, to push back against the rising numbers of new immigrants. The early movement focused mainly on Irish Catholics.

- Much of the nativism was derived from a belief that immigrants would accept lower wages for jobs primarily held by the "native" city-dwellers who were trying to earn a living wage from their factory work. There was also a belief that Catholics were loyal only to the Pope, not the US government.

- The most infamous of the nativists were the Know-Nothings. This group organized the burning of Catholic churches and violent riots aimed at immigrants. Their name is derived from their secretive nature and the instructions to group members to state that they "knew nothing" when asked about group activities.

- Know-Nothings expanded their hatred to include free Blacks, as well as Asians, and they also lobbied for strict quotas to be placed on a variety of immigrant groups. They had limited political success, and as the Civil War started, their pro-slavery stance began to erode their credibility in the North.

- As the "new' immigrants began arriving in America, nativist thinking spread rapidly across the US, and various nativist groups pushed the US government to pass laws limiting immigration.

Link it Back

Government officials often took an indifferent stance on nativist groups. Many politicians were concerned about the overpopulation of cities caused by immigration, but those same politicians recognized the significant labor needs caused by the rapid expansion of US industry.

Link it Forward

Nativism rose again in the 1920s as the US isolated itself from European troubles that were evidenced in WWI.

NATIVISM — THE ANTI-IMMIGRATION MOVEMENT

Chinese Exclusion Act: 1882

- In 1882, Congress passed the Chinese Exclusion Act, which suspended Chinese immigration for ten years and made Chinese immigrants already living in the US ineligible to be naturalized as citizens. Congress admitted that the law was passed to ease the concerns of nativists who expressed the need for "white purity" and wage security for white workers.

- After a failed attempt by Chinese Americans to repeal the law, the act was renewed in 1892, and Chinese immigration was completely abolished in 1902. These acts did a great deal to diminish the Chinese population in the US.

- Chinese people in the US remained ineligible for citizenship until 1943.

- This is NATIVISM.

Link it Back

The first major wave of Chinese immigrants came to the US in the 1850s to take part in the California Gold Rush.

Link it Forward

Many of the workers who helped build the Transcontinental Railroad were Chinese immigrants. The Exclusion Acts hurt railroad companies who found themselves in a labor shortage by the turn of the 20th century.

CHINESE EXCLUSION ACT: 1882

Gentlemen's Agreement: 1907

- Starting as early as the 1860s, nativists led an anti-Asian immigration movement on the West Coast. By 1904, the Chinese Exclusion Acts had done a great deal to reduce the Chinese population, so Japanese American and Korean American immigrants were specifically targeted. Many of these immigrants came to the US without American passports, because they entered the country from Canada or Mexico.

- In 1907, the San Francisco School Board set up a segregated school for Asians. Nativists applauded the decision while the Japanese Prime Minister was outraged at the treatment of former Japanese citizens. Some in Japan urged the prime minister to cut trade with the US.

- Looking to maintain good relations with Japan, President Theodore Roosevelt asked the San Francisco School system to lift the segregation. In response, Japan agreed to no longer issue passports to the US to Japanese citizens. They also stopped allowing Japanese immigrants to enter the US after receiving passports to another nation. This "handshake" deal allowed the US and Japan to continue their trade relations.

Link it Back

Anti-Asian nativism was rampant on the West Coast for 40 years prior to the Gentlemen's Agreement. This nativist attitude hampered the railroad industry, which relied heavily on Asian immigrants who labored to lay down track and blast away rock to build tunnels in the mid-19th century.

Link it Forward

The segregation of San Francisco schools paled in comparison to the forced internment at Japanese American relocation centers during WWII. These centers were established because Americans thought Japanese Americans presented a potential security risk during the conflict with the Japanese in the Pacific.

Gentlemen's Agreement: 1907

The Emergency Quota Act: 1921 / National Origins Act: 1924

- In 1921, the federal government passed the Emergency Quota Act, which lowered the total number of immigrants without specifying the immigrant's nation of origin.

- This law was seen as a major victory for nativists groups, including the KKK, who lobbied to limit the number of "new" immigrants coming to the US from the Middle East, Asia, and southern and eastern Europe. The law represented a significant turning point for American immigration policy, a turn toward stricter limits.

- In 1924, Congress passed the National Origins Act which lowered the number of immigrants admitted from any country annually to 3 percent of the number of residents from that same country already living in the United States. The 3 percent number was based on the 1910 Census.

- The National Origins Act was reauthorized in 1929, and further reduced the number of immigrants allowed into the US.

Link it Back

In many ways the Quota Act was simply a reflection of the extreme isolationist policies of the Post-WWI era. This was part of President Harding's call for a "Return to Normalcy." Immigrants, Catholics, Jews, union members, and socialists were associated with foreign issues and problems. Foreigners and foreign ideas were not welcome.

Link it Forward

Tragically, in the 1930s, the Quota Act and the Origins Act prevented a number of Jews, persecuted in Nazi Germany, from gaining entry into the US and escaping the wrath of Adolf Hitler.

EMERGENCY QUOTA ACT: 1921 / NATIONAL ORIGINS ACT: 1924

Made in the USA
San Bernardino, CA
10 May 2016